Ellen Nauman

About the Author

Renowned psychologist, speaker, and columnist DEBRA
MANDEL, PH.D., has twenty-plus years experience
specializing in helping individuals and couples with
relationship struggles, depression, anxiety, stress,
childhood mistreatment, eating disorders, addictions,
and general life concerns. She is the author of *Your Boss
Is Not Your Mother* and *Healing the Sensitive Heart*. Dr.
Debra is a regularly featured relationship expert on
numerous national TV and radio programs, making
high-profile appearances on *The O'Reilly Factor*,
MSNBC, CNN, *Headline News*, and several reality
shows. She's known for uniquely combining sensitivity
with a "take charge" approach to life, giving audiences
new inspiration for positive change.

Dump That Chump!

From Doormat to Diva
in Only Nine Steps

{ A Guide to Getting Over Mr. Wrong }

Dr. Debra Mandel

HARPER

NEW YORK · LONDON · TORONTO · SYDNEY

HARPER

In order to protect the anonymity and privacy of my clients, I have changed
their names, circumstances, and other identifying information. Any similarity to actual people is coincidental. In some cases, I've created composites
that closely resemble the experiences of real people. The information in the
book is meant to educate, illustrate, and offer hope to the reader. It is in no
way intended to be a replacement for professional help.

FIRST EDITION

Designed by Joy O'Meara

Library of Congress Cataloging-in-Publication Data is available upon request.

ISBN: 978-0-06-121330-4

ISBN-10: 0-06-121330-6

07 08 09 10 11   ID/RRD   10 9 8 7 6 5 4 3 2 1

I dedicate this book to all the women who have so candidly shared their stories of heartache with me and who have accepted my advice on how to break ties with a chump. Without their willingness to bravely challenge themselves to take new action and experience positive results firsthand there would be no book. Their courage will forever serve as an inspiration for other women who feel hopelessly stuck in their dead-end relationships to finally see a light at the end of the tunnel.

Bravo!

Acknowledgments

$\mathcal{I}$'m incredibly fortunate to have so many supportive and caring friends (new and old) in my life. I hope you know who you are and how much I appreciate your gifts of love. Were it not for your sticking by me through thick and thin, I'd probably still be moving from one chump to the next, losing all faith in romantic love. So please accept my heartfelt thanks for letting me cry on your shoulders and encouraging me to keep on going!

I wish to give special thanks to my agent, Linda Konner. You've listened to all of my ideas (many of them hardly worth repeating), never once expressing doubt in my ability to come up with a great topic. You've continually inspired my creativity, even during the times when I've lost momentum. I would never have made it to the big leagues were it not for your tremendous support and encouragement!

To my editor, Sarah Durand. Your enthusiasm has been delightfully contagious, and I cherish your support for this project. I love your fresh ideas and gentle style in giving feedback. Thank you so very much for your acceptance and accessibility. Working with you has been truly awesome! May we have the opportunity to create many bestsellers!

To my entertainment attorney, friend, and partner, Rod Lindblom. Having you in my court has been such a great comfort. Your humor and wit have kept me smiling and laughing through many disappointments! Thanks for being the calm in the storm and for always picking up my spirits. We'll have our own show yet!

To my daughter, Tiffany, the most precious gift in my life. Though I want to protect you from all the pain and hardships you may encounter, I know I must refrain and allow you to experience everything life has to offer. My greatest joy comes from watching you grow into a beautiful young woman with a strong personality and purpose. I know you will live life to the fullest, and I'll forever be proud of you!

To three very special children: Rachel, Remi, and Delainey. My life would not be complete without each one of you. I hope you will never have to endure the suffering that comes from loving a chump. But if you do, remember I'll always be there to comfort you, with lots of tissues at hand!

To my sister, Cheryl; my dad, Al; and my stepmom, Dora. Your love and support have been endless. You've been there through all my ups and downs, never once losing confidence in my abilities. Thanks for always making me feel like a star! And special thanks to Sue and Jim, whose continued support has truly made my life easier!

To my deceased mom, Laine. Though we rarely saw eye-to-eye, I learned many valuable things from you. I only wish we'd had the chance to become closer before your passing. I hope you're in a happy and tranquil place, free of all your suffering.

Acknowledgments

To my best friend, lover, confidant (and favorite home-improvement guy), Chris. Thank you for caring so much about me and for your unwavering belief in my success. You've been an invaluable grounding force in my life, especially during those gruesome times when I've lost sight of the important things in life. I always cherish your love, even when I'm cranky or irritable. You are my rock and my anchor. I love you!

Last, but not least: to all of my former significant others. Many of you would certainly qualify as chumps (though, of course, you won't be the ones reading this book), but most of you were good guys who just weren't a good fit. I'm grateful to have been able to experience many different types of relationships so that I can really appreciate true love. There's no end to what we can learn from our intimate bonds. Thanks, guys, for all of the lessons of love.

With my deepest appreciation to all of you!

Contents

Contents

Dump That Chump!

Introduction

Women from all walks of life find themselves in dead-end relationships, knowing they're never going to be happy by staying—yet they can't seem to leave. No, they're not ugly or undesirable; nor are they vapid airheads unable to function independently. Rather, they're smart, attractive, and interesting! Yet they don't behave as such. Often, even long after they recognize their guy isn't going to change, they'll continue making excuses for his bad behavior, trapped by feeling sorry for themselves, or by fear of being alone. Most tragically, they're held hostage by the misinformed belief that they'll never find someone who will treat them any better.

Mind you, this is not a small group I'm referring to; rather, this description applies to millions of women. Over the course of my professional and personal life, I've met hundreds of women suffering from this condition. Frankly, far too many women sell themselves a whole bunch of crap by believing that this is simply the nature of the beast. Many women will say, "Men are who they are and we women must lower our expectations, lest we wish to be alone for the rest of our lives." Or worse, they'll say things that make themselves the cause of their guy's obnoxiousness, like, "Oh, if only I were [*fill in the blank*: nicer, prettier, skinnier, smarter, blah, blah, blah], he wouldn't be such a jerk." They believe they can't do better, and thus rationalize his bad behavior as acceptable.

The truth is the guys they're stuck with are CHUMPS! And these men (if you can even call them that) aren't going to change. In fact, the longer one stays with a chump, the more chumpy the chump becomes—because he knows he can get away with it. There's simply no incentive for him to change. But that doesn't mean his partner has to put up with him.

I say it's high time this self-destructive behavior by so many wonderful women comes to an end. Women need to stop wasting their time settling for less than they deserve. They must stop putting up with the chronic disappointment and hurt that inevitably come along with staying with guys who mistreat them. Though these women don't believe it, good men do exist out there—men who will treat them right.

Of course, it's hard to break these patterns. Believe me, I know. In fact, after many painful relationships with my own set of chumps, I think my personal experience may even better qualify me as an expert on this subject than my years as a practicing psychologist—even though I've specialized in dating and relationships for more than twenty years. Plus, this syndrome of dating chumps cuts across women from all walks of life. So please know that if this describes you, you're in good company.

Let's face it. Even though the women's movement and all the hoopla about equal rights have put us firmly on the map as a recognizable species, we women are still being taught that we're second-class citizens and that our needs don't matter as much as our man's needs do. Just turn on the tube for a few hours, open a newspaper, or examine the gender of those at the helm of major businesses and you'll see that men still largely hold more power and receive more respect than women do. (Don't get me wrong. I'm certainly not encouraging women to feel victimized, nor am I bashing men. I am just making a point that it's understandable that many women do not take good care of themselves in their personal, intimate lives.)

God forbid we women put ourselves on an equal playing field with men, claiming our own needs first. Then we're liable to be labeled "selfish." And I don't know about you, but I've never experienced that label as complimentary. So, if we become strong enough to break ties with a loser, in order to avoid such a noxious appraisal, we often spend months—if not years—idealizing the chump, blaming ourselves for the relationship's failure, and unable to move forward. Or we follow the well-intended but not very effective advice of many self-help resources that tell us to spend enormous amounts of time and energy being angry—as if demonizing the bum will actually make us feel better. What we're not being offered are tools for how to get over these bad matches and move on. No revenge, no sulking—just letting go!

Yes, I know this may sound harsh. But anyone who knows me would tell you I'm far from insensitive and I'm actually very compassionate. (Of course, you might find a chump or two whom I've left behind who may beg to differ. But, consider the source! ☺) Actually it's because I have such empathy for women stuck in these futile cycles of staying hooked on the wrong guys that I can be so matter-of-fact. Remember, I've been there myself many a time. So if my tone sounds harsh, I encourage you to stay with me for a while and understand that I'm coming from a loving place—although my approach is a kind of tough-love one.

I, along with so many other women, unfortunately had to learn how to dump a chump the hard way: by a painstaking process of trial and error. But it doesn't have to be this hard. Women simply need a better, far more efficient way to stop being doormats, get on with their lives, and create space for Mr. Right!

So how do you dump a chump with only minimal suffering? In the chapters ahead, I give you a unique approach proven to work with the hundreds of women whom I've helped break up with chumps and never look back. And it doesn't take nearly as long as you might expect. In fact, the notion that it takes half as long to get over a breakup as was the length of the relationship is ludicrous. We don't have to dwell on bad relationships once we fully embrace the fact that we deserve better. It's just a matter of getting back our self-worth—or developing it in the first place if it's been lacking. And, hey, it's just par for the course that Cupid is going to goof once in a while. This just doesn't have to be such a big deal.

Once we recognize that a relationship isn't going anywhere, we can lick our wounds and move forward, paving the way for a much better experience the next time Cupid comes calling. But like anything important, we have to build the muscles to develop the stamina to break free.

Using my years of clinical expertise specializing in relationships (and of course my years of wisdom acquired by dating chumps), I bring you a nine-step program to dump that chump once and for all and finally make room for Mr. Right. Featuring dozens of real-life anecdotes, quizzes, checklists, practical tools, and exercises, the book will get you into shape for passionate, nurturing love with a good guy. You'll learn to distinguish chumpy behavior from that which is workable, and you'll learn what drives you to stay with such a loser.

Since chumps come in a variety of sizes and shapes, I also describe several incarnations, from the most to the least toxic, and how to handle each one. *Dump That Chump!* will also teach you how to stop crying over spilled milk and get over feeling victimized once and for all so you can become a better target for love's arrow. With this guide, you'll learn to change the beliefs that keep you stuck and to challenge yourself to take actions that effectively combat the temptation to rekindle a dead fire.

Clearly, tons of books deal with breakups. But I think you'll find that this one stands out among the others by (1) highlighting your strengths rather than focusing on your weaknesses, (2) building on your capacity to laugh and love, and (3) providing you with hands-on tools to quickly dispense with any residual hurt and anger. Plus, *Dump That Chump!* will boost your confidence and teach you to become the captain of your own ship, empowering you to hold out for a good match and never again settle for love from someone who doesn't behave lovingly. You'll learn that *you* hold the key to ending your suffering and to finding happiness. Unlike other self-help sources, this book dispels the myth that we need to spend time grieving for our loss before we can move on, that we can't successfully start new relationships until all the grieving is done.

If you follow all the steps in *Dump That Chump!*, you will come to accept that, while sometimes Cupid goofs, you *can* quickly thrive in a new relationship. The program, therefore, is concise, packing a wild punch and curing the distress in no time. This book is for you if:

+ you have had one or more experiences of staying stuck with a chump

+ you want an effective, prescriptive method for getting through the pain quickly
+ you desire a better relationship
+ you have grown tired of romantic patterns that keep you from finding a thriving relationship

So if you believe you're currently with a chump, have just recently dumped or been dumped by one, then please read on. Or, if you're not with a chump right now but you've been with one in the past, you can also benefit from reading this book, especially if you're returning to the dating world after a hiatus. After all, it never hurts to employ an ounce of prevention.

Please keep in mind, however, that everyone heals at her own pace. You must take into account a whole slew of things that can affect how quickly you're able to move on, such as: your temperament or personality; how long you've been in your relationship; how many previous times you've been in relationships with a chump; your age, maturity level, and level of family and social support; whether or not you've had kids with the guy; and your intensity of attachment. Thus, I can't absolutely guarantee a specific time frame. However, I believe you'll discover that by following the steps you'll be well on your way to a pretty good base, if not complete resolution, sooner than you now imagine.

Take Carrie and Ed, for instance. They shared seven years, two kids, and completely intertwined lives. It took Carrie several months to fully recognize the joy of being divorced from her ex. As you can imagine, with court and custody battles, she had to deal with a lot of ongoing exchanges with Ed, at times tripping her up in her mission to move on. But she got there eventually—and far more quickly than she would have had she not come across the tools outlined in this book.

In contrast, Barbara and Kirk had only been dating for six months when the light went on alerting Barbara that she was with a chump. Luckily for her, this was her first time having fallen for a jerk, and she had awesome friends and family. So she was able to plow through the program in fewer than six weeks.

Keeping all this in mind, please do not judge yourself if you take longer, or if you need extra help from a counselor or support group in addition to this guide. Don't be ashamed if you need a boost from others. Just stay focused on your mission and you will see results!

If you're someone who has been fortunate enough to have escaped the painful trappings of a chump or if you have never even encountered one, you can still benefit from reading this book. Most likely you have at least one friend or loved one who's in a sinking love-boat. In fact, I don't think I've ever met a woman who hasn't had at least one story to tell about a chump either she or a friend has dated or, worse yet, married. Even most guys I know have a story or two to tell about a friend involved with a chump. This syndrome runs rampant in the female population. So don't put this down too quickly. You may wish to offer this guide as a gift; or you can read it yourself and pass along some pearls of wisdom you discover that may help wake up your friend to her reality. After all, a true friend can be enormously soothing and helpful in times of romantic doom. And while it's not your job to disengage someone from a toxic relationship, you may very well be the inspiration she needs ultimately to make the break.

Warning: As a final note before we plunge ahead, please be aware that this book is not sufficient for those of you who might be involved with an abuser. And I don't use this term loosely. I mean someone who physically batters, rapes, or victimizes others in various ways. While all abusers are usually chumps, all chumps are not necessarily abusive. The abuser-chump is addressed in Chapter Three, but this book is not intended to help those who are in danger. If this is the case, please seek professional help immediately and appropriate shelter. You can always come back to the book as a resource for further healing—but you must first create safety!

Chapter 1

Cupid's Mission

Though you may be eager to immediately dive into the program for how to dump your chump, as your coach and guide, I can't in good conscience recommend you launch into it without first helping you build a foundation. Thus, while it might be tempting to skip ahead, I strongly discourage jumping forward until you understand my framework for a healthy intimate relationship. Otherwise, even though your motivation might be strong to get rid of the bum, without an appreciation for the true benefits of tossing him out the door, you will have a hard time successfully reaching your goal, and you'll leave yourself vulnerable to even more pain and suffering—which I assume you've already had plenty of! Hence this chapter is dedicated to providing you with information concerning the elements that draw us to relationships, why we're prone to staying too long in those that aren't working, and what we have to look forward to by getting out of a bad relationship.

Of course, if you believe you can't wait a little while longer, you're welcome to skip ahead, but you might find yourself missing a good laugh or two that will hopefully bolster your confidence to do the dirty deed of breaking up with your chump. So, if you can stand it, bear with me for a bit longer and gain the fortitude necessary to move forward. After all, breaking up is never an easy task. And with a chump the process can be especially brutal, since they often very cleverly use their charms to repeatedly reel you back in.

So for right now, sit back and enjoy the story of Cupid and why it's relevant to dumping a chump.

Cupid—the God of Love

So who is this mythical creature known as Cupid? Is he man or boy?

And does he really have the market cornered on love?

Though I'm certainly no expert on mythology, quite frankly after my review of Cupid's tale, I think the guy's been highly overrated. First off, he runs around or he glides (I'm not really sure how he travels) half-naked with wings on his shoulders and a bunch of arrows on his back. Second, in many photos, it appears he hasn't worked out in some time, if ever. (Probably a downside to having wings.) Finally, by today's standards, he's quite dorky-looking, not very manly, and he certainly lacks style. And, as though that's not bad enough, he doesn't even look like an adult, yet he's been granted license to be in charge of some very potent weapons. (Last time I heard, getting pierced by an arrow is very painful.) If you really think about this little mythical mystery, he's more akin to a misbehaving hormonal preteen than to a vibrant male lover, let alone a mature intimate partner. Nevertheless, he's certainly gotten a lot of airtime for his expertise in matters of the heart.

As the story goes (though you could read hundreds of different versions), the little guy was sent by his envy-stricken mom, Venus (a famous Roman goddess, also known as Aphrodite in the Greek version), to make Psyche, the awesomely beautiful mortal, fall in love with a monster. The goal was to get Psyche off the market, hence eliminating any threat to Venus's status as the most attractive creature. Of course, Cupid couldn't pull off his mission, and he accidentally pierced himself with his love arrow, making himself fall for the glorious Psyche. (Rather clumsy, don't you think?) They do get married, but Psyche never actually sees Cupid. In fact, she thinks he's the monster, and he can't tell her otherwise, because if anyone gets wind that Cupid has disobeyed his mom, he's really in for it.

So they maintain this façade for a while—with Psyche never actually seeing that she hasn't married a monster. Her sisters, who also believe she's with a monster, coach her on how to get him into the light so she can cut off his head. Of course, when she finally does get an *in vivo* glimpse of him, she thinks he's pretty hot. But once exposed, he's gotta split to avoid Mama's wrath—so he deserts her. This puts Psyche in a tizzy and, no longer being able to stand the abandonment, she seeks Venus's forgiveness. (Though keep in mind, while this may sound like a romantic tragedy, Psyche's actually quite shallow: she's chasing after a guy she knows nothing about other than what he looks like.)

Venus, who's completely emotionally disturbed, makes Psyche jump through hoops impossible for any mortal to achieve. Every time Psyche takes on one of the futile challenges posed by Venus (which she's supposed to handle solo), Psyche breaks the rules and accepts unsolicited help from various other gods. But

Venus always catches on—the paranoid that she is. You'd think that as desperate as Psyche is to get back her beloved Cupid, she would at least try to comply with the directions she's been given. (Talk about shooting yourself in the foot.)

Finally, to Cupid's credit, he convinces his mom that Psyche's the gal for him, and he wins her approval. Psyche then drinks some potent cocktail and becomes immortalized as the renowned Goddess of the Soul. Yikes, what a way to get promoted!

Granted this is my own, certainly distorted interpretation of the myth—and I'm sure that many would see Cupid's plight in a much more favorable light. But based on my analysis, I'm only impressed by a whole lot of dysfunction: deceit, betrayal, secrecy, and other less than ideal conditions. Okay, so Cupid does eventually stand up to his mom, but come on! Lucky for Psyche, she wasn't killed in the process. Would you really want a guy with all that baggage in charge of your love life? Not to mention, if Cupid was truly less than a fully matured adult, as he generally appears, then with today's laws, Psyche would be considered a child molester. And the alternative isn't much better. In other words, if Cupid was a full-fledged adult man (though a pretty wimpy one), then doesn't his behavior sound a lot like that of a stalker? I don't know about you, but neither of these options seems very appealing, and certainly not my idea of the makings of a healthy relationship!

Okay, so maybe I'm being a bit harsh. Most of us don't really know or remember the sordid details of the legend of this little love god. More commonly, the mere mention of Cupid conjures up romantic images of true love. And many use his name to describe the process of falling in love once struck by his arrow. In fact we'd all be rich if we had a dime every time Cupid's name has been used in association with love.

But even if we see Cupid in a positive light, it's important to understand that an ancient mythological tale doesn't make for a very realistic model for how to have a healthy relationship, especially in modern times. And many women have made the mistake of holding onto Cupid's arrow as proof that they should continue to try to salvage a bad relationship. The fact is that Cupid sometimes goofs! And sometimes in a really big way. So maybe, just maybe, the important lesson is that chemistry simply isn't enough. Nor is love, for that matter. We also have to have other fundamentally necessary ingredients like respect, maturity, and the ability to hold each other's needs in high regard (qualities that are in short supply in a chump—no matter how attractive he may be). Otherwise, we're doomed to passionate starts and very gruesome endings.

Putting Cupid in Perspective

Okay, so no more ragging on Cupid. Instead let me put his mission in perspective so you'll see how it relates to your situation.

When we meet a guy and wholeheartedly fall for him, that's Cupid at work. If chemistry calls, then we feel the butterflies in our tummy and that druglike euphoria of being on cloud nine. Nothing matters but getting his next phone call and seeing his face when he comes to pick you up for the next romantic night out on the town. You can talk all night with endless interest and energy. No matter how much time you've been spending with him, it doesn't seem like nearly enough. And the chemistry becomes even more enticing if he reciprocates these feelings. Within a short time, you're both professing everlasting love, believing these wonderful feelings will never end. After all, "How could it fizzle, when he's so perfect?" you think.

But, uh-oh! The magic spark begins to fizzle. And once the fizzling begins, Cupid bails, and you're on your own. Cupid's onto making another love connection. He doesn't stick around to see whether the chemistry plays out in long-lasting commitment, let alone whether you're being treated right. Basically, his job is to light the fire and bring the two of you together. Whether you stay together, and how happy you are, is out of his hands. That's strictly up to the two of you.

Mind you, in all relationships, the initial charge fades a bit. The brightness of his smile grows a little dimmer. He's not so perfect after all. But then again, neither are you. And, in fact, he may not have changed a bit. You're just no longer seeing him through a soft-focus lens. Both of you get cranky now and again, and both of you step on each other's toes unintentionally. But this isn't such a tragedy if what emerges is a solid relationship with a loving guy. Because even though the sparks have faded a bit, if there's plenty of security, love, trust, respect, and compatibility the love is kept alive, and ultimately a new breed of passion emerges. With this deepening of love, new magic ensues, based in reality rather than in hormonal love potions.

I'm thinking, however, that since you're reading a book on how to dump a chump, things haven't turned out so sweetly. The honey, once so sweet to the taste, now seems more like petroleum jelly. I'm sure you're acutely aware that the honeymoon period doesn't last forever. In fact, if you're with a chump, you may not have received any of the initial goodies or, at best, you received them only for a very short while. There's even a good chance you may not have had a honeymoon period to speak of. But I'll assume that one of the main reasons you've stayed with your chump is because you once fell madly in love with him. He was probably like a beautiful peacock spreading a lovely array of colorful feathers. But within a relatively short period of time, usually six weeks to six months after the initial rush, he started to resemble something much more like an ostrich. But you can't let go. You're still waiting for the peacock to return.

Well, girlfriend, I hate to break the bad news to you, but I seriously doubt Mr. Peacock will ever return. By and large, once those feathers close up, you might as well consider them permanently plucked. Unless of course he's on to his next prey; then it's amazing how quickly those feathers might just reappear.

There is one exception to this rule: if your chump really does love you, even though he's clueless about how to behave, he may—under condition of your threats to abandon him—be able to reclaim his feathers and do another fanning. But, generally, as soon as he's comfortable believing you're going to stick around, he'll be back to his same shenanigans. So essentially, once you've passed through the magic of the honeymoon period, if you don't like what you see in front of you, it's only going to get worse. Even if he does make some noises about being willing to change, you're likely to be too resentful of how much you've already put up with to notice or be satisfied with the changes.

Tori, a twenty-three-year-old grad student, fell head over heels for Jacob. He, a twenty-seven-year-old up-and-coming professional, swept Tori off her feet during the first three months of their dating. He took her out to great restaurants, brought her flowers, and asked her about her favorite terms of endearment. He led her to believe that she was his dream come true. He even went so far as to charm the pants off her friends and family (though, thankfully, not literally). Great fairy-tale start. But unfortunately for Tori, the ending was more like a nightmare.

Shortly into their passionate courtship, Jacob showed signs of being a chump. Tori, too in love to pay attention, dismissed these signals and found herself getting more deeply attached to him despite his dramatic change of colors. For example, he stopped calling her just to say hi and would get annoyed when she'd call him, even though he initially claimed to love her daily check-ins. And if she called him at work, he would really fly off the handle, despite the fact that it was he who had told her he was reachable 24/7.

As if these changes weren't bad enough, Jacob would also hog all of Tori's personal time, getting irritated if she wanted to get together with some of her friends for dinner during the week. But he would think nothing of calling her last minute to say, "Something very important has come up," and break their plans. Of course, later she discovered that many of these important date-breakers were nights out at strip-clubs with his boss! Jacob had also assured Tori that he wasn't like his buddies who couldn't peel themselves away from the tube, yet he'd watch sports all day on Sundays. Come to think of it, he was pretty much glued to the tube whenever he wasn't working, which was also more often than not.

Mind you, Jacob might have been a good match for someone with similar values and interests. But once he displayed his true colors, it became quite evident that he and Tori shared virtually nothing in common. But did Tori dump him upon this discovery? No, despite being a very intelligent young woman. Why? Because she was so deeply invested in being part of a couple, she stopped behaving smartly and instead became caught in the web of romanticizing a jerk. She wanted to believe that these signs were out of character for Jacob, when in reality they were indicative of his true character. Sadly, months went by with Jacob behaving badly before Tori realized that she was being taken for a very destructive ride with this guy. Yet like so many of us who have endured relationships with chumps, Tori put far too much stock in Cupid's arrow, dismissing her better judgment and allowing herself to be mistreated.

Fortunately, Tori eventually came to her senses and worked hard to build the stamina she needed to dump her chump. It wasn't easy for her to make the break, because she was so ridiculously attracted to Jacob. But she finally realized that who he initially purported to be was a far cry from who he actually turned out to be, and his courting behavior had simply been a ploy to get her hooked. Ultimately, she was able to stave off what would have most likely been a life sentence of misery by struggling through the intense pain of finally breaking free from him. Thank goodness!

Karen's story highlights yet another tragedy with a different twist, though fortunately also with a positive ending. Whereas Tori's chump never demonstrated any awareness of what a jerk he could be and essentially played on Tori's self-doubt so she would believe her misgivings about him were entirely her own creation, Karen's guy, Mark, occasionally voiced seemingly heartfelt contrition for his actions and made repeated promises of better behavior.

Mark's pattern was such that he would treat Karen like crap for as long as he could get away with it. He wouldn't make her a priority; he'd pick on her body, calling her "chubby" (knowing she was very sensitive about the ten pounds she'd gained after spraining her ankle); and he'd generally disregard the things she told him were important to her. After numerous violations, she would put her foot down and threaten to leave if he didn't change his ways. Fearful of being left, Mark would come to her with his tail between his legs, saying how sorry he was for hurting her and promising to be better in the future. He never hit her, but in many ways his behavior resembled that of an abuser—i.e. he'd beat her up emotionally and then beg for forgiveness. And as soon as the remorse phase wore off, he'd emotionally batter her all over again. Understandably, because Karen was so in love with Mark, she held onto anything that gave her hope. Unfortunately his assurances all turned out to be empty promises. He had no intention of ever changing. His pleas for forgiveness were simply meant to placate Karen so she wouldn't leave him. No one really ever understood what she'd seen in him to begin with. But, like so many others struck by Cupid's arrow, Karen mistakenly equated chemistry with love.

Karen regrettably wasted a lot of her time—more than two years—in a constant state of waiting for "potential." Not until she caught Mark red-handed in a lie did she finally realize he had just been playing on her kindness and generosity of spirit, especially her ability to forgive. Mark had no real intention of ever changing his ways.

Once Karen finally gave Mark his walking papers, she quickly regained her self-esteem and was able to minimize the hold he'd had on her. By taking active steps like the ones outlined ahead, within six months she had moved on to a new relationship with a far more hopeful future.

Both Karen and Tori had different experiences, but their process was very similar. Both were with a chump, and both were the by-products of Cupid's goof. Though they each had to learn the hard way, they did eventually discover that however potent the chemistry can be, they needed to hold out for much more than an erotic elixir if they were ever to have a truly loving and passionate relationship.

Please keep in mind that I'm in no way negating the importance of chemistry. Quite the contrary. I don't think any intimate relationship can really work out long-term without a hefty dose of lust and the "I gotta have him now" kind of feeling. But we can't give this all the power. While it's a necessary condition, it's certainly not sufficient on its own, especially since the passion in a relationship goes through many ebbs and flows.

Now let's move onward to understanding love.

What Does Love Have to Do with It?

I'm probably sounding like quite the love-cynic by now, trashing Cupid—our love-legend—and seemingly devaluing the importance of chemistry. But au contraire! I consider myself to be a true romantic. As I just mentioned, chemistry is of the utmost importance in getting a relationship off the ground. And, like chemistry, love is of great importance. But as I'll show you, love can't be the only driving force behind a relationship.

What is love anyway? I think we'll all agree it's a terribly difficult word to define since it's so difficult to measure. And each of us most likely has her own unique definition of it. But for simplicity's sake let's say that love is a very strong affection for another and/or a passionate attraction and desire.

Love can be sexual or erotic, or it can be platonic and friendly. It can be parental or the kind that's shared between siblings. But unlike relationships between friends, parent and child, or siblings—where one particular kind of love dominates—in a healthy intimate relationship we will often feel all of these different varieties of love toward our partner at one time or another. And it's our ability to experience so many different kinds of love that makes a romantic relationship so special and distinct from all our others. But loving someone in terms of the emotions we feel doesn't always translate into loving behavior. And this is the problem with putting too much stock in love and not enough stock in how the love gets expressed through actions.

If how a person demonstrates or expresses his/her love doesn't feel good, then it really doesn't matter whether someone claims to be in love or not. For instance, Lisa preferred to have some quiet time when she got home from work. Not so much space that she was abandoning her mate, but just enough for her to discharge the stress of her day. She asked Chad for about fifteen minutes to chill, and he agreed to give it to her because he loves her. But five minutes into her requested time-out, Chad would routinely start badgering her with questions. In his mind, he was trying to connect with her. But do you think she was feeling loved at that moment? No! Why? Because Chad kept breaking their agreement. He was actually behaving quite selfishly, not lovingly, since he wasn't demonstrating respect for their agreement. Not that this example is such a big deal, or grounds in and of itself to qualify Chad as a chump, but it does highlight how behavior has a bigger impact on whether we end up feeling loved than words alone do.

I make the distinction between feeling love for someone and demonstrating loving behavior because I can't tell you how often women stay in relationships because they believe their guy really loves them, despite his behavior suggesting otherwise. After all, if he says the words "I love you," how can he possibly be a chump? Because actions speak louder than words. And in the detailed descriptions of these relationships it usually becomes crystal clear that these women don't *feel* loved. The point is that being in love is not enough. The feelings must get translated into loving actions.

Michele, a thirty-year-old vibrant mother of two, finally got fed up with her chump, Nathan, after six years of marriage. Nathan was exactly that guy whose actions never lived up to his words. To this day, he's clueless as to why Michele left him. He still believes he did all the right things. He called her from work every day just to say, "I love you." He sent flowers when he'd been a jerk and he wrote sweet nothings in cards on her birthday and their anniversary. But he rarely ever lived up to his agreements. He was Mr. "Make It–Break It," meaning he'd make a promise and never keep it, or he'd say he was sorry and then five minutes later do the very thing he'd just apologized for. For instance, they had both agreed to certain chores and responsibilities connected to maintaining the house. But, lo and behold, something always seemed to come up that was more important than what he'd promised Michele.

We're not talking about once in a while negligence or laziness; we're talking about perpetual letdowns of a serious nature. Several times Nathan would promise to pick up their kids from daycare, but he'd be out slamming cocktails with his coworkers instead. The underlying message was that his life was more important than anyone else's. Truth be told, he never should have agreed to be a family man. He seriously lacked the maturity necessary to take on these responsibilities.

It was very hard for Michele to dump her chump, especially since she felt so guilty about breaking up the family. But once she faced the reality that he was never going to change, she realized she'd be far better off raising her two children alone than having to raise three, since one was actually an adult and not her child at all!

Michele's story is but one of hundreds I've encountered where a guy professes love, but surely doesn't act very lovingly. And Michele, like so many others, stayed far too long in her relationship with Nathan because of early dysfunctional models of love she'd learned in childhood. So let's now turn our attention to two very important questions: Where do we get our models of a loving relationship? And how do we develop a healthy model if ours is wrought with dysfunction?

How We Create a Healthy Model of Love

Understanding the origins of our internalized models of love is critically important with regard to our ability to get out of a bad relationship and to prevent ourselves from ending up in the same boat the next time Cupid comes calling. Without this awareness, we run a very high risk of repeating the same cycle over and over again, chronically choosing guys who don't treat us well.

Certainly it's possible for you to have had a one-and-only experience of being with a chump—as a fluke lapse in judgment. Or possibly you were seduced by a con artist whom no one, even the most emotionally healthy of all, could have escaped. However, it's largely been my experience that hooking up with chumps can easily become a pattern if we're not careful. Or you may notice that it already has. And in order to fully rid yourself of any chump residual, the pattern needs to be consciously broken. So while you might be one of the few who is truly in a foreign land (this is your first-time chump experience), don't be hard on yourself if you know or soon discover that this has actually been a familiar pattern—a different name, place, height, weight, eye color, etc., but the same bad feelings all over again. But you needn't despair. Once you're conscious of this pattern and why it exists, you can break it once and for all!

So where do we get our models of love and how does this relate to ending up with a chump? We learn our ideas about what constitutes loving behavior by what we observe in other people's relationships and from the relationships we've experienced with others. As you may already be aware, our models of love start from birth and continually get morphed along the course of our development. And these models come from all over the place, including significant caregivers (parents, teachers, aunts, uncles, grandparents, nannies, etc.), media role models (television and movies), and religious institutions, to name a few.

Even fairy tales, with their happily-ever-after endings, influence our concept of love—though we never really get to see how the romance actually plays out beyond the kiss on the wedding day. You know—Cinderella, Snow White, the Little Mermaid, to name a few. And as I've already described, even mythology, e.g., our ever-popular tale of Cupid, has some effect on our developing minds with regard to models of love.

While there are many sources from which we gain our love notions, for most of us, our earliest experiences with our significant caregivers have the biggest impact on how we form our concepts of love. (Of course, our temperament also interacts with these experiences.) And everything builds from there.

Though we certainly don't want to point the finger exclusively at our childhood role models, there's just no escaping the fact that how we were treated early on has a big influence on how we define love and on the kinds of partners we end up choosing during our adult years. Not to be overly simplistic, but by and large if we had less than nurturing relationships with our caregivers and/or we witnessed dysfunctional intimate bonds between influential adults (e.g., between our parents), we run a higher risk of becoming magnets for chumps. And even when we recognize that we aren't going to get our needs met by these types of guys, we stay anyway or at least far longer than serves our best interests. Why? Because if we weren't properly nurtured or well cared for by those responsible for our development we're likely to be plagued by low self-esteem and unhealed emotional bruises, hence becoming doormats. And we will often fail to recognize that we deserve anything better than the kind of treatment we're familiar with.

Does this mean that we're doomed to a life of bad relationships if our childhoods were less than adequate? Absolutely not. In fact, who we end up with is entirely of our own choosing once we have become independent adults. And we shouldn't pin our choices (good or bad) on anyone but ourselves. To be a healthy adult and have a solid, intimate relationship, we must accept responsibility for our own choices and behavior. So while we mustn't be too hard on ourselves, especially if we've internalized a distorted image of healthy love, we need to fully accept responsibility for our present choices. It's through this accountability that we can finally be free to have thriving, intimate bonds.

So putting aside any shame or blame, I want you to try to wholeheartedly embrace the notion that if you were left with any holes in your self-worth as a by-product of your development, it's your job to fix them. Once you fill up the holes with self-love, self-respect, and self-acceptance, and let go of old unhealthy messages of what love is, you have a far better chance of choosing wisely the next time around.

I will give you lots more tools throughout the book for inner repair, but for now try to simply understand and accept that your original models of love have possibly skewed your intimate partner choices, and they may need to be modified. Take a moment and ask yourself if you think this idea may have some merit. If so, then pay close attention to how your old internalized ideas about love may be reenacting themselves in your present relationship.

Sibelle's relationship offers a great example of how early role models impacted her choice in an intimate relationship—unfortunately, with a chump.

Sibelle, a twenty-five-year-old account manager, came to see me after recognizing that her relationship with Pat closely resembled that of her parents. Basically, it sucked! Just like her dad had treated her mom badly, Pat treated Sibelle like a second-class citizen. He disregarded her opinions about things and always tried to control where and what they did together. If Sibelle had a contrary point of view, Pat would flat-out tell her she was wrong. Pretty amazing that such a successful, intelligent, and educated woman could be wrong so much of the time!

Sibelle's mom had stayed married to her dad out of a sense of duty and obligation, constantly making excuses for her husband's bad behavior. On occasion, Sibelle would ask her mom why she put up with her dad. Mom would reply with things like, "Oh, your dad works so hard. He doesn't mean to be such a grump; he's just tired. I know he loves me." So this became Sibelle's concept of a "loving" relationship. It's no big surprise that she was attracted to Pat. Sibelle would also make excuses for Pat, especially with regard to his temper. She believed that Pat got as mad as he did at her because of how much he cared about her. What she needed to come to understand was that Pat's temper had nothing to do with her and everything to do with him lacking anger-management skills—among many other things.

So if this speaks to your situation, just know that you are in good company. And, if possible, have hope and faith that, regardless of your previous experiences, you can develop a healthy model of a loving relationship—one that will serve you well!

The Makings of a Healthy Relationship— The Foundation for Mr. Right

So what qualities are necessary for a healthy union? Below is a list of what I see as the basic essential ingredients for a successful intimate relationship. I've subdivided my list into two sections: the qualities that should be present and those that should not be. As you move through your pain and regain your confidence, you will add your own personal touches to the list. But for now, just use this list as a guide.

The presence of:

◆ mutual respect
◆ passion for each other
◆ ability to embrace differences as long as they are not outside your core set of values
◆ kindness and consideration
◆ similar sense of humor
◆ ability to communicate feelings, even those perceived as negative
◆ sensitivity to vulnerabilities

The absence of:

◆ contempt
◆ desire to humiliate
◆ disregard for the other's feelings
◆ intent to harm or make feel bad

Keep in mind, contrary to popular fairy tales, even if you find your prince, he's going to have flaws—just as you, the princess, have your shortcomings. There are natural ebbs and flows in even the best relationships. But in a healthy relationship, far more often than not, you should be feeling good about yourself, liked, and respected by your mate for the person you are, and treated lovingly. You should never again settle for less.

At this point, I encourage you to take a deep breath and focus for a moment or two on a positive image of the relationship you desire. You will expand on this later, but for now, get out a journal and jot down a few of the qualities you now know are non-negotiable—i.e., you simply have to have these qualities in a mate in order to be happy. Your list may include some of the qualities possessed by your chump (after all, he may not be all bad), but be sure to include on your list those things you've been longing for that aren't present in this relationship.

Now let's move on to Jasmine's story in the next chapter so you can get a full picture of what's in store for you.

Chapter 2

When Cupid Goofs

Jasmine's Tale of Woe

To better understand the havoc of being tied to a chump, let's meet Jasmine. Her story depicts, in detail, the full process of engaging and disengaging from a true-blue chump. Hers is a story of transforming devastation into triumph. And, hopefully, her tale will help take away any shame or embarrassment you may be carrying for being in your situation—ultimately providing hope for new beginnings and a much happier romantic future.

As you read on, keep in mind this is not a competition. You may believe your situation is far worse than Jasmine's and be tempted to dismiss any similarity. Or, you may think your experience doesn't even come close to Jasmine's suffering and then conclude that you're just being a baby or making a mountain out of a molehill. Neither of these interpretations will do you any good. Instead, try to refrain from quantitative comparisons. Don't minimize the importance of your suffering should you believe that Jasmine had it far worse. And vice versa. If you believe you are in an even worse predicament than Jasmine, don't convince yourself that there's nothing for you to relate to. Again, there isn't one type of chump. They come in all varieties. There's simply not enough space to be able to give an example of each. But I do hope that Jasmine's story reflects enough commonality that you will feel encouraged to be able to dump your chump.

I take extra care in stating these precautions because women attached to chumps notoriously believe that no one could possibly understand their particular situation. If this describes you, you're likely to focus only on how this story *doesn't* apply to you. For example, if you're married to a chump, you might discard the relevance to Jasmine since she never married hers. Don't rule out commonalities because the surrounding variables such as age, marital or parental status, or years together, may be quite different.

Though you're probably in a lot of pain (emotional and possibly even physical) and you may feel very alone in your suffering, others who have been involved with chumps do share many similarities—again maybe not always in terms of the content (e.g., in how his chumpiness gets expressed) but certainly with regard to the process (i.e., the feelings of despair, isolation, hopelessness, desperation). So please read with a focus on Jasmine's process of transformation rather than on the details of her relationship.

Jasmine's Story

Jasmine, an intelligent, dynamic, and very attractive twenty-seven-year-old nurse, had been seriously dating Derrick for two years before she came to see me in therapy. Derrick, a great-looking, well-built thirty-year-old sales rep, had completely stolen her heart. She loved him more than anyone else she'd ever gone out with, and within a short period of time she anticipated a fairy-tale ending of living happily ever after. Boy, had he poured on the charm. But despite Derrick's initial princely presentation, he turned out to be a big chump. He fully exemplified the guy who knew how to get his catch, while remaining utterly clueless about how to actually maintain and nurture a committed relationship. He gave the word "immaturity" a whole new meaning. What a loser! But he certainly didn't seem that way in the beginning.

Derrick and Jasmine first met at a birthday party for one of Jasmine's closest girlfriends. Derrick had just moved into town and a friend of his had invited him to the party so Derrick could make some new acquaintances. Or as it later came out, Derrick's friend had actually said, "Hey, man. Come check out this party with me—there's supposed to be a ton of hot babes!" (Classy, huh?) This information, however, wasn't revealed to Jasmine until she was well into the relationship.

Jasmine and Derrick had each been mingling with different sets of people for some time before they laid eyes on each other. But once they did, one would think it was pure magic. Of course, what Jasmine hadn't known was that Derrick had been on a mission to collect as many telephone numbers as possible. (Note: I do believe Derrick was genuinely attracted to Jasmine, but, as you'll soon see, his later behavior clearly demonstrated that he had no real interest in being a good relationship partner.)

As Jasmine described it, "Our chemistry was like two volcanoes simultaneously erupting." Derrick appeared equally smitten—fumbling on his every word and acting almost geeklike in the cutest sort of way. He even tossed his own drink on himself after Jasmine accidentally spilled her drink on herself, just so she wouldn't feel embarrassed. "How endearing!" she thought. Their meeting could easily have been a screenwriter's dream scene for the opening of a romantic comedy. And Cupid, of course, was seriously pleased with himself—sitting back, gloating at his matchmaking success. (But remember: Cupid doesn't stick around.)

After several hours of intense conversation oblivious to others in the room, the party came to a close and Jasmine and Derrick felt the push to leave. Naturally, because of their intense attraction they did not want to separate. Had hormones been the sole drivers of their cars, they'd have been in bed together within minutes. But Derrick, acting as a "gentleman," politely asked Jasmine for her number and said he'd call her the following morning. Without hesitation, Jasmine gave it to him, and she parted with eager anticipation of the next day's sunrise.

Derrick was true to his word. He phoned her bright and early the next morning, gushing about what a fabulous time he'd had and wanting to know the soonest possible opportunity when he could see her again. Jasmine, too, couldn't wait to be back in his presence, and they set their first date for that very evening. Candlelit dinner, dancing, and two lattes 'til dawn. The romance had officially begun!

Jasmine and Derrick hung out together almost every night for the next several months, except of course on Fridays, Derrick's one sacred night out with the boys. He wined and dined her, frequently sending flowers, chocolates, and love notes. Jasmine, being a people-pleaser, tried anything Derrick suggested for fun. She found that she enjoyed doing whatever he wanted as long as she was doing it with him. He, being the outdoorsy-type, took her river rafting, skiing, and fishing—three activities she'd never done before meeting him.

She didn't mind that she was always the one adjusting her schedule to fit his. She never complained or said no to any of his plans because she wanted to make him happy. She understood he loved the adrenaline rush and he was inviting her into his world. She'd become his favorite playmate. What more could a girl want? (Of course, the fact that he didn't provide any training even in the riskier sports didn't faze her in the least. She simply chalked it up to his adventurous personality.)

This dynamic duo tore up the town for several months—Jasmine in bliss. By the sixth week of their whirlwind experience, Derrick said, "I love you," and waited in eager anticipation for Jasmine's reciprocation. And he got it. She blurted out the words right back at him. And soon after that they started having sex—unprotected—yikes! But to them it didn't matter since they were already talking about being together forever. (Not a good move, the unprotected sex part, as you'll soon discover.)

Things went along seemingly great for another month or so. Then the deterioration began when Jasmine had an outbreak of an STD virus, herpes. She was very ill for a couple of weeks (common for women with a first occurrence), and she felt utter betrayal. At first when she confronted Derrick, he denied knowledge that he carried the virus. But after a great deal of arguing and seeing Jasmine's anguish, he rose to the occasion and actually confessed that he'd had it for many years. (What a guy!)

Jasmine was outraged. She wanted to dump him right then, but he convinced her of his undying love and promised her they would be together for always. He told her she didn't have to worry about infecting anyone else because there would never be anyone else. (Mind you, this is not to say that people with herpes can't have intimate partners but, rather, how important it is to share such information with any potential lover so he or she can make the decision about whether to go for it or not. Jasmine was never given the information.)

Feeling scared and damaged, Jasmine became even more dependent on Derrick and fearful of losing him. Against her better judgment and the advice of her trusted friends, she dismissed her own feelings and forgave Derrick. She convinced herself that he had good reason for not having told her the truth when she'd asked him about STDs: he had said he was scared she would leave him and he would have been too devastated. Like so many women caught in the snare of a chump, she didn't want to see how much she was being manipulated and how wrong he was for her!

While the whole herpes thing was probably by far the worst of Derrick's offenses, causing harm to Jasmine on multiple levels (emotionally and physically), it certainly wasn't his only misdeed. His once-a-week boy's night out soon turned into three or four nights a week. And his charm and charisma were no longer directed at her.

Derrick also became a perpetual flirt. Though he probably had always been one, he had initially managed to censor his urges while he was first courting Jasmine. The "I only have eyes for you, babe" comments bore no resemblance to his behavior anymore. He couldn't even spend one minute focused on Jasmine before some other woman walking by would command his attention. But, once again, because of her love for Derrick, Jasmine chalked these insults up to his being a guy. And she convinced herself that he'd either grow out of this behavior or he'd surely change his ways once he knew he was hurting her. Not!

Jasmine completely dismissed how devalued she felt. She believed her own hurt feelings were the by-product of old insecurities—and hence ultimately her own responsibility to fix. Yes, building self-esteem was her job, but come on—let's cut her some slack. How can an orchid thrive in a desert, let alone even grow properly? Sadly, Jasmine kept hanging on.

After their first year together, despite his multiple offenses, Derrick and Jasmine moved in together. The few times Jasmine threatened to break up with Derrick, he would do a one-eighty, showing her glimpses of his initial behavior. He'd engage in a few more activities with her and bump up the volume on his terms of endearment. Basically, he'd throw her a bone or two, and she'd fall for these gestures hook, line, and sinker—feeling grateful that she had stayed committed to him. But these visits back to the early days of their romance were quite short-lived. Almost always he'd revert back to his chumpy behavior within just a few days.

To make matters worse, Jasmine caught Derrick surfing porn sites late at night. When she'd tell him she felt hurt by this, he'd make her feel like she was acting crazy. "All guys look at porn. It's no big deal," he'd say. Though she continued to yearn for his touch, he became less and less interested in her physically and not at all available to her emotionally. Not a big surprise, since he was channeling his desires through smut!

As time went on, the traces of self-esteem Jasmine came into the relationship with completely dissolved. She became increasingly insecure, feeling totally unattractive. She also isolated herself from her friends, spending most of her free time fixated on contemplating ways to make Derrick desirous of her. Before long, Jasmine was in a full-blown depression. She'd gained more than twenty pounds, having turned to food for comfort since Derrick virtually ignored her. Rather than focusing on what an ass he turned out to be and planning her escape, she instead wondered why *he* stayed with *her*, fearful that he would dump her.

Before long, Jasmine began suspecting that Derrick had taken his cyber-infidelities to a new level—i.e., cheating with a real partner. And she was right. One day she came home from work earlier than expected, and there he was sucking face with another woman, he and she both half-naked! He even had the nerve to tell her that it wasn't what it looked like. Yeah right! Finally Jasmine realized Derrick was just using her. That's when Jasmine had finally had enough. She wanted out—for good! Enough was enough! But she had no idea how to actually break free.

Jasmine's Journey Through Dumping Her Chump

Jasmine arrived at my office looking like she'd seen a ghost, been hit by a truck, and just been diagnosed with cancer all at the same time. It was obvious she'd been crying for days, with a nose redder than Rudolph's and eyes as swollen as cracked walnuts. She'd not been sleeping enough, if at all, and she could barely tell her story without breaking into uncontrollable sobs. I felt so bad for her, knowing the depths of her pain and the magnitude of her self-hatred. (Remember: I, too, had been involved with many chumps—far more often than I care to admit. So I certainly wasn't judging her!)

Upon meeting Jasmine in a state of utter despair, I wanted to put my arms around her and rock her like a little baby. I wanted to tell her everything would be okay and that she had nothing to worry about. I felt an urgency to protect her from further harm and shelter her from her pain. But I knew that acting on these impulses would ultimately keep her stuck and do her an injustice. Rather, I had to resist mothering her, and help her discover and embrace her own inner strength.

Within minutes, it became crystal clear to me that while Jasmine needed a hefty dose of soothing, she also seriously needed confidence-building along with a total behavioral and emotional overhaul. She needed new tools to help her change her entire system of how to approach relationships and her beliefs about love. And given how low she'd gotten, we both understood this would not be an easy process. Yet despite how broken she seemed, I completely trusted that Jasmine could and would definitely pull herself out of her despair and reclaim her life. And I also knew that she would quickly be able to attract a much better suitor and no longer be a magnet for chumps.

When I first met Jasmine, she blamed herself for everything. "Why didn't I see this coming?" "How could I be so stupid?" "Am I really so bad?" "Who will ever love me?" "How can I ever trust again?" These were some of the many self-deprecating questions she asked. She also tortured herself with endless "if only" statements. "If only I had been sexier, he wouldn't have gone for anyone else." "If only I'd had a lively or more outgoing personality, he'd have been more interested in me." "If only I hadn't done [x, y, z: blah, blah, blah], he never would have . . ." You get the picture. She'd convinced herself that she bore sole responsibility for the demise of the relationship, as if somehow she'd created Derrick's chumpiness. It never occurred to her that Derrick was a jerk and that it was *he* who was responsible for his bad behavior.

Granted, Jasmine hadn't been a saint. Who is? She acted bitchy now and again. Sometimes she didn't do exactly what she'd promised, e.g., she'd forget to make a reservation for his golf game or she'd be late for their evening's event. But hey, oftentimes her relationship blunders were actually because she was too busy thinking about his needs. For instance, often she'd be running late because she was spending far too much time working on her makeup, trying to look her best—afraid she'd disappoint him.

Jasmine also had her ups and downs. As is true for many of us, sometimes Jasmine wasn't in the mood for sex. You know—PMS, hard day at work, too many things on her mind, etc. That's right—the common stuff. Or she'd be thinking too much about her work. (Not to mention dealing with the repercussions of Derrick's continually insensitive behavior.) But being the caring, nice person she is, she would sincerely apologize when she hurt his feelings and take responsibility for her occasional blunders or unintentional insensitivities. Plus, she was generally thoughtful of Derrick's needs and feelings. Her behavior hardly qualified her as the female equivalent of a chump—as in BITCH!

While many of us are taught the saying "It takes two to tango," meaning that both partners share in the responsibility of a negative dynamic, this phrase shouldn't be taken to mean that each always contributes equally to the dysfunction. In fact, I would hands-down describe Derrick's behavior as objectively more hurtful than anything Jasmine had ever done. And some of his offenses were truly heinous, such as failing to disclose a known STD.

Despite Derrick's far more toxic actions, Jasmine continually judged her own imperfections as though they held the same weight as his. And when she verbalized how sorry she was for her "stuff," he never helped to ease her conscience. Rather, he'd actually rub them in her face. "Hey, if she wants to rationalize her own minor infractions as excuses for my blatant offenses, far be it from me to talk her out of it" seemed to be his overall stance.

What Jasmine didn't see was that she wasn't at all to blame for Derrick's immaturity or inconsiderate behavior. Nor was she responsible for his bad choices. And she certainly didn't have the power to force him to change. But what she did have control over was her own actions. And she needed to come to understand that only she could make her life better.

With her priorities straight, she was on her way to dumping Derrick out the door for good. Once she began viewing Derrick in a reality-based light instead of through rose-colored glasses, her emotional heaviness lightened up quite a bit. And she was even able to have a sense of humor about the whole experience.

During the weeks ahead, Jasmine discovered that she held no responsibility for Derrick's bad behavior, regardless of his tendency to blame her. She also came to recognize that holding him accountable for his behavior was not being "mean." And although it was enormously difficult for her to pull this breakup off, she bit the bullet and told him to "get the hell out of her life for good." She eventually stopped making excuses for his actions and soon realized he was not worthy of her time.

At first, as is common to women who have been trapped in the lair of a chump, she stubbornly insisted that they should part as friends. But before too long, she was able to toss this wish, along with him, right out of her mind. She came to recognize that true friends don't lie to and/or cheat on each other. And while she didn't need to make him an enemy, she certainly didn't need to invest any more energy in nurturing a relationship with him.

With her newfound courage, Jasmine gave Derrick his final walking papers. Of course, he didn't believe her, since she'd attempted a few permanent departures in the past. But this time she was committed to following through because she was finally able to accept that his cycle of making promises of better behavior were about as valuable as a drop of water from the Pacific Ocean.

Not surprisingly, given Derrick's complete dismissal of responsibility for his actions in the relationship, it should come as no big surprise that he fought her on who should move out of their apartment. He of course tried turning the tables on Jasmine, making her feel as though she was being the villain and, if she wanted out, then she should leave. Initially, Jasmine went head-to-head with him for the apartment. But once she took a step back and reclaimed her better judgment, she soon realized that she'd be better off starting fresh in a place without any memories of him.

This decision was not without a hefty price. Since they were equal partners on the lease, she had to pay for two extra months of rent while also paying for her own place. Understandably, she was tempted to stay the extra two months to save the money, as the move put a strain on her financially. But once she did a cost-benefit analysis, she soon understood the emotional price she would pay would far outweigh any benefits she'd gain economically by staying through the lease. Basically, she realized if she worked a few extra shifts at the hospital and passed on a few extraneous purchases such as name-brand shoes and fancy dinners out, she would be able to almost break even *and* begin her road to healing much more quickly. Though this may not be the best move for everyone, it was certainly the best choice for her. She also understood that while there were consequences to each of her choices, at least she had choices. She wasn't as trapped as she once perceived herself to be!

Next, Jasmine needed to take a look at her childhood history to see whether she was carrying around any negative messages about love. She needed to uncover any unhealed bruises that may have played a role in why she chose Derrick to begin with and discover why she stayed with him for such a long time in a state of misery. These were not obvious at first, since Jasmine actually felt she'd received plenty of love from both her parents. But as she revealed more details relating to her family dynamics, it became increasingly more apparent that despite her parents' good intentions they exhibited some very destructive behaviors concerning love.

Jasmine lived with both her mom and dad (Maureen and Bill) until she was twelve, at which time her parents divorced. She and her older sister remained with Mom, but Dad continued to play an active role in their development. In some ways her parents never really disentangled from each other, despite each having remarried. (Keep in mind, though, Bill and his second wife divorced after only three years of marriage.)

In her early years, Jasmine had observed her mom and dad in constant battle. Though her dad was far more aggressive than her mom ever was, her mom would certainly contribute to the battles with passive digs. In fact, as Jasmine recounted, it almost seemed as if her mom wanted to piss off her dad, as she would often "forget" to do her assigned tasks. As a stay-at-home mom, Maureen was in charge of managing the household. But somehow something else seemed to always come up so that Maureen didn't have the time or energy to finish the housecleaning or get to the market. In hindsight, it's as though she were rebelling against her husband in the only way she knew how. Any attempts to vocalize her unhappiness about anything only led to defensiveness and yelling, so she went through the back door instead.

Jasmine's parents weren't physically abusive, nor were they neglectful. And because they tried their best, Jasmine had a hard time seeing that her childhood experience would have any negative impact on her later choices in mates. But in order to claim responsibility for her life as an adult she needed to see how the way she was raised clearly shaped her thinking without *blaming* her parents. Otherwise, without understanding the impact of the messages she'd unknowingly internalized, she'd continue to be a ripe target for more chumps.

Jasmine's parents were never able to remedy their differences to make peace. No matter how hard they tried, they simply couldn't seem to get along for more than a day or so. Jasmine recalled many occasions when she would flee to her room in tears wishing her parents would learn to be nice to each other. Sometimes she would watch television programs depicting family interactions, and she would long to be swallowed up in the set, merging into the on-screen family. She loved her mom and dad, but she remembered often thinking they were really nuts.

On several occasions, her dad, Bill, would move out of the house, threatening to never come back. Jasmine would become terrified, fearing that they would starve without him. Her mom had never been so good at taking care of any financial matters, so how in the world would she be able to take care of the kids? But lo and behold, within a week or two he would always return—making some perfunctory gesture of an apology—asking Maureen for another chance. While Jasmine would feel hopeful upon his return, his gestures clearly turned out to be meaningless attempts to manipulate his way back into the family. (Even following the divorce, Bill would make efforts to return, and Maureen would give it another go—their reasons were never quite clear.)

The few months following Bill's return would always be blissful. The family would do lots of fun things together (picnics, bowling, and amusement parks) and Jasmine would feel intense relief and hope for better days. But inevitably these days of bliss would cycle back around to tension and animosity, and Jasmine would regain her growing sense of despair.

As though Jasmine didn't have enough on her plate already by dealing with intense feelings, her mom added to her burden. Though not with the intention of harming her daughter, Maureen would often seek comfort from Jasmine—even ask her for advice on how to handle her husband. Since Jasmine had always been such an empathetic and sensitive child and Maureen was in constant emotional pain, Jasmine was a natural outlet for her woes. Sometimes Jasmine would even forgo fun events with her friends in order to be Mom's consoler when Dad would disappear. And at the time, Jasmine even welcomed this role, as it made her feel special and important in the family. However, she ultimately came to realize that being her mother's "therapist" had many negative consequences.

Jasmine's dad, Bill, was really a piece of work. Not that he didn't love Jasmine or have good intentions as a father. But he simply didn't have the understanding or the resources to make this happen. He meant well. But, hey—if I repeatedly step on your toe because I'm not watching where I'm going, your toe will still be throbbing even though I didn't mean to hurt you. And the pain doesn't go away until I stop stepping on it. Bill simply wouldn't stop stepping on Jasmine's emotional toes.

So despite Bill's intentions, he failed in many regards. He never took responsibility for his behavior. No matter what had transpired between him and his wife, Bill would end up feeling like the victim. And he had no trouble bending Jasmine's ear on many of his lonely nights post-divorce with his woes of how Maureen lost the best man she would ever have. To make matters even worse, Bill often bad-mouthed women in general, calling them "gold diggers" and "users." As you can imagine, this did not help Jasmine develop very high regard for herself or for her gender.

There's a lot more to Jasmine's background than I've accounted for, but needless to say, she grew up with a very dysfunctional image of love and relationships. As you can see, how her parents had treated each other and how they each had treated her had shaped her concept of love. And it shouldn't be all that surprising that she would have stayed with a guy like Derrick.

Derrick and Bill share many similar features. To name a few:

+ They both act like victims and fail to take responsibility for their own behavior.
+ They lack the maturity necessary for healthy intimate relationships.
+ They have a general disregard for females.
+ They don't learn from their mistakes and continue to blame others when things don't work in their favor.
+ They lack the courage to be honest with themselves and others.

Jasmine's fixation on making the relationship with Derrick work also had a lot to do with what she'd emulated from her mother's behavior. Just like Maureen had done with Bill, Jasmine too quickly dismissed Derrick's bad behavior or made excuses for it. Though Maureen did in fact ultimately pull the plug with Bill, Jasmine witnessed many years of a push-pull relationship—one that never got any better, despite repeated promises of change. Also, because Maureen had inappropriately confided in her daughter, Jasmine developed tolerance and compassion for others, but at the expense of learning healthy boundaries for herself.

All in all, while Jasmine certainly had many fortunes in her childhood such as a good education paid for by her parents, traveling adventures, and other enriching experiences, she did not have the best role models in the love department. Hence she was left with a number of holes affecting her judgment when it came to matters of the heart. But once she was able to successfully connect the dots between her unhealed childhood bruises and the dynamics in her relationship with Derrick, it became much easier for her to have empathy toward herself and get rid of the shaming/blaming voice inside her head. These realizations allowed her to carve a path for a better journey the next time around.

In the weeks ahead, Jasmine also learned new tools for how to quit pining over Derrick and rid herself of unnecessary sadness and anger. She came to understand that letting go of her relationship with Derrick was much more of a gain than a loss. Now she'd have the freedom to ready herself for a truly loving, intimate partner who would treat her with respect and kindness, qualities so lacking in Derrick.

Most important, Jasmine learned how to soothe herself. Like many people who stay in dead-end relationships with a chump, Jasmine was masterful at taking care of other people's needs but had little experience attending to her own. And because she gave so much energy away to other people, she became more and more dependent on Derrick to fill her up. The less he would give, the more she would feel that something was wrong with her. She couldn't see that there was nothing wrong with being thirsty. The problem was that she kept going to an empty well for water.

Since Jasmine often judged her self-value based on whether others approved of her, she had a particularly hard time identifying her own personal methods to self-soothe. She had to come to understand that what feels good to one person doesn't always feel soothing to another. Hence she needed to fine-tune her desires, even if they seemed odd to other people. As long as she wasn't harming someone, including herself, then anything needed to be okay. With this new level of self-acceptance, Jasmine discovered all sorts of possibilities.

Some things on her list still required a reliance on others' cooperation—for instance, hugs and reassurance from others. But that was okay because she also came to recognize she didn't need to have these fulfilled only by a lover. Okay, so a hug from a friend is not really the same as from someone you have the hots for, but it can certainly do in a pinch. In essence, Jasmine realized that she could rely on multiple resources to feel soothed.

Most important, Jasmine began to rely on her own self to provide soothing.

Before long, she discovered that she could praise herself and treat herself with kindness and that by doing so, she felt a lot better about herself most of the time. And, through consciously ridding her mind of negative, critical self-talk, she discovered that she actually liked many things about herself. She also revised her beliefs about her importance in the world. For instance, she came to understand that she did not need a relationship in order to have value as a woman and certainly she didn't need a man in her life if he didn't treat her well.

Despite having absorbed a second-class mentality through her family and social upbringing, Jasmine grew to embrace the idea that her needs mattered as much as anyone else's. The loss of a relationship didn't have to mean she'd be alone forever. While she certainly desired to be in love and in a committed relationship, she came to appreciate that this was a preference, and not a need.

Of equal importance was that Jasmine no longer felt like a victim. She could see that she was ultimately responsible for creating the love life she deserved. Once she accepted that she was the captain of her own ship, she could steer it in the direction of her choice. And she would never have to settle for a less than wonderful mate.

Once Jasmine revised her thinking and improved her self-concept, I encouraged her to exaggerate her indulgence toward herself. I knew full well that Jasmine would never become a self-centered arrogant bitch (something she had feared people would see her as should she focus more attention on herself). Rather I wanted Jasmine to fully experience her gains and lavish in self-glory. She resisted at first, but soon she caught on and allowed for the celebration of who she is. She threw a party for herself, honoring her being. It wasn't even her birthday. Some of her friends thought she was a bit nuts since Jasmine had never demonstrated such self-appreciation. But they quickly got over that, and a few of them followed suit with their own annual self-indulgent party.

Now Jasmine was ready to reenter the dating scene. This time around, however, she understood the value in taking her time and really getting to know someone before fully investing her heart and soul. I didn't encourage her to be guarded or defensive, just cautious and alert to any yellow or red flags. She understood the peacock phenomenon and how we all tend to put our best foot forward in the beginning of a romance, but we don't generally see someone's true colors until at least a couple of months into dating someone. She also had a much keener sense of how to present herself and not just adapt, chameleon-like, to a guy's desires.

As can be expected, Jasmine kissed a few frogs along the way. But because of all the changes and growth, she didn't stick around for very long once she had a pretty good sense that who she was out with wouldn't be a good match in the long run. At times she doubted that she would ever be able to find a good partner—but she stuck it out and kept the faith.

Within a year, Jasmine met a guy she really liked. Using her new tools and resources, she went a lot more slowly. Much to her surprise, as time went on he actually appeared to be an even better and better match that she'd ever dreamed possible. She had almost the reverse experience that she'd had with Derrick. This new guy, Gavin, was a keeper. And while I can't say they lived happily ever after because it's only been a couple of years, I can certainly say that she's on the right track. Sure, they have their ups and downs, as all couples do. But on a scale of zero to ten on chumpiness, with ten representing "maximum chump," Gavin rates a zero. Way to go, Jasmine!

So there you go. Jasmine dumped her chump, and you can too. Now let's move on to determining if you're truly with a chump. Though I'm pretty sure you already know. Then we'll get to the steps of actually letting him go, pushing through the painful feelings and memories, and building the resources you need to start afresh with hope and joy. That's right—you need to transform from doormat to diva!

Chapter 3

Are You in Love with a Chump?

*I*n some ways this chapter is merely a formality since all that really matters is if *you* think your guy is a chump, not whether he fits the criteria I've outlined below. But once again, because women who attach to, and stay with, chumps often suffer from a great deal of self-doubt, it can be very validating to see in print a full description of what constitutes a chump. Of course the risk you take is that I will not have adequately defined all avenues of chumpy behavior, and I in no way want to add to any confusion you may already be experiencing. So I caution you as you read ahead not to rule out that you're with a chump if I've failed to highlight any examples or descriptions that fit your situation.

Having said that, I think in certain situations it is important to get other people's opinions about what truly constitutes chumpy behavior. Not because your own opinion or experience lacks enough weight but because, with more information or a stronger sense of self, what once seemed like chumpy behavior may no longer feel so bad. Let me explain.

If you're plagued with low self-esteem and a tendency to feel victimized, you may harshly judge your partner's behavior as bad news, when it may simply just be bad news for you—a sort of mis-fit, if you will. For instance, you and your mate have different goals and you can't seem to come to an acceptable compromise. Or you may actually misperceive someone's behavior as truly harmful or abusive, when in fact if you felt stronger and more empowered, the behavior might only qualify as mildly annoying, but certainly not something scary or hurtful.

Katie, a highly sensitive thirty-two-year-old research assistant, had been physically and emotionally abused as a child by her father. And during her late adolescence and twenties she dated many men and had a couple of very significant relationships, lasting several months to a couple of years. Some of the men she dated turned out to be violent like her father had been toward her. And she knew that she didn't want to re-create that cycle.

Katie eventually sought some therapy and developed enough inner strength to finally say "NO" to abuse. But as so many people do once they feel they've made some progress, she cut off her healing journey prematurely. And in doing so, she concluded that all men are assholes and not to be trusted. "Get what you can out of them, but never be vulnerable again" was her new mantra. As a result she stayed stuck, having swung her pendulum in the opposite direction, believing all guys were up to no good. She sold herself a belief that if she wanted to have a relationship she'd simply have to settle for the least possible evil.

Katie didn't stop dating or searching for her Mr. Right. But she had no tolerance for differences whatsoever—believing that if her mate disagreed with her in the slightest way or even raised his voice a little bit, he qualified as an abuser. She couldn't see the difference between verbal abuse and passion/animation. Understandably, because of the abuse she'd endured from her father and several men she'd dated, she'd reached her limit of mistreatment. She'd taken too much for too long and wasn't about to take anymore. And in order to prevent future abuse she overgeneralized to keep herself feeling safe. But what she didn't see was that this mentality continued to keep her a prisoner and unable to distinguish abuse and objectively intolerable behavior from basic differences or annoyances.

Katie sought my help to breakup with Cory, a thirty-one-year-old bartender who was taking part-time classes toward a business degree. Katie had been seriously involved with Cory for the past year, and she wanted to get married so she could start having kids, but he wasn't ready yet. Because of his "lack of commitment" she concluded that he was just another "user." Thus, she thought she was wasting her time and should move on. But what I discovered later on was that Cory actually really loved Katie and envisioned a long future with her—but he wanted to finish school (about two more years at the time) and *then* do the marriage and baby thing. He wanted to have confidence that he could be a good provider. Though Katie said this didn't matter to her, he was a bit old-fashioned and needed to build his self-confidence before taking that next big step.

Based on Katie's description, however, Cory certainly seemed like quite the chump at first. According to her, he wasn't that into her and he was taking her for a ride. But when I asked her for some examples of behaviors she found so offensive, all she could name were general feelings of not having enough of him. "I just don't feel like he cares that much about me," she'd say. Or, "He doesn't want what I want and he makes me feel bad about it." But being a curious sort of gal, I just didn't find this to be enough information. Not that I was out to disprove her assessment, but the ducks weren't lining up. And I've certainly been guilty of having unreasonable expectations of people based on having felt cheated of enough love and attention at one time or another.

After many chats with Katie, gathering of her history, and understanding more about Cory and his background, I thought that maybe Katie was being a bit hasty in her decision to dump Cory. It seemed plausible that because she didn't feel good about herself, she was placing unreasonable demands on Cory and wanting more from a relationship than would be healthy for anyone. Not that he couldn't learn a few things about how not to add insult to injury, but by and large, he seemed like a pretty decent guy. And I just wasn't in sync with her perception that he was such a chump.

So rather than going right into the program of how to dump her chump, I instead suggested that I meet with the two of them in couples counseling to see whether they might actually stand a good chance of a happy future together. As it turned out, Katie came to understand that she was replicating many of her old emotional bruises from previous relationships, and she needed to heal these. She realized that just because her dad and other guys had been cruel to her, it didn't mean Cory would be too—all men weren't alike. And she learned that she had to fill up her own aching for love and approval with her own resources. Basically, she came to accept that it was she who had to improve her self-worth and learn to love herself. Then, and only then, would she actually be able to experience love coming from someone else.

In our individual sessions, Katie came to realize she may have prematurely booted out a few fairly good prospects—i.e., those whose differences from her might have been workable and not at all threatening to her well-being. This was a slippery slope at first since Katie tended to feel shame whenever she discovered something about herself that put her in a less than ideally favorable light. But, fortunately for her, she managed to plow through her shame and see that she could change her pattern and truly distinguish a chump from a potentially good guy.

Once Katie took the necessary steps to heal herself, she was able to see Cory more accurately, discovering that he wasn't mistreating her at all. She ultimately opted to stay with him, and he proved to be very true to his word. After a couple of years, he did in fact finish school and they planned a lovely wedding.

In Katie's situation, she projected malice onto a guy who turned out to be pretty okay. But the reverse also commonly occurs—a tendency for some women to continually sugarcoat a behavior and deny how bad it really is. Based on what you've endured in your previous relationships with family and intimate partners, you might have developed such an unusually high tolerance for damaging, abusive behaviors that you don't even recognize blatant mistreatment. As a result, you may not even think your guy's behavior is all that bad, even though you chronically feel like a loser when you're in his presence and you're constantly in emotional pain. Plus, everyone around you thinks the guy's a monster. Often with this scenario you see other people having relationships where the partners treat each other with kindness and respect, but you may rationalize that you don't deserve this goodness, or you may believe that you actually provoke, even cause, the hurtful behavior.

For instance, Marjorie and Craig had been together for eight years, married for seven, with a three-year-old girl, Annie. Prior to Annie's birth, Craig had been an asshole to Marjorie, but Marjorie accepted this as her lot in life. Others would ask her how in the world she put up with him. And she would generally shrug her shoulders and say, "Oh, that's just Craig's nature; he can't help it." She'd add, "I don't mind so much. He doesn't hit me or anything. I just let his moods pass." Like her own dad, she had a passive approach to relationships, not expecting a whole lot and being grateful just to have someone. In her family, her mom was the tyrant, criticizing everyone else and blaming the world for her own foul moods.

Craig was a total control freak, with no awareness of how difficult he could be. Early in their relationship, he'd disguise his controlling behavior by presenting it as "protectiveness." He'd show up at Marjorie's apartment in the wee hours of the night, just to make sure she was all right. In reality, he didn't trust her (for no apparent reason), and was checking up on her. He bought her a membership to his gym, explaining that he wanted to have more opportunities to see her. But the real story was that he wanted to know what she was doing at all times. He'd throw away her stash of Oreo cookies because he thought she'd be clogging her arteries, but really he was trying to monitor what she ate because he feared she'd get fat. (Mind you, she was skinny as a rail. He was the one who was twenty or so pounds overweight.) She of course didn't know any of his hidden motives and simply thought his attention to her was a sign of how much he cared about her. The worst part was that he would never cop to how controlling he was and would turn everything on her as though she were being difficult.

Craig also had managed to hide his temper until they got married. It's as though he had it all planned. Once he secured the goods, then he felt entitled to do whatever he wanted to them. She became his possession, and she learned it was much easier to just go along with his demands than to fight him and encounter his rage.

Plus, she'd had good training in this department, having walked on eggshells around her mom. Whenever Marjorie would make small noises about being unhappy (only to him, never to the rest of the world—where she always kept on a happy face), he'd tell her they'd have a better life if only they had children. So she got pregnant, and things were better for the first year or so after Annie's birth.

Craig was nicer to Marjorie, and he loved having a baby who adored him. Not that he would change diapers or comfort Annie when she was cranky or tired. But when she was quiet, he'd play with her and give her lots of cuddles.

But once Annie became a toddler, doing toddlerlike things (e.g., throwing little tantrums, leaving toys all over the place, and tossing food on the floor), things took another drastic turn for the worse. While Craig's obnoxious behavior had once been solely directed at his wife, he was now aiming it at Annie, as well. He started yelling at Annie, calling her stupid, and even disowning her as his own child. Sure, some parents playfully tell their mate, "Hey, honey, *your* kid is acting up again," but you know they're just kidding, simply trying to make light of some of the frustration they're feeling about parenting. But not Craig. He really sounded like he meant it.

It took a little while of witnessing this behavior and trying to intervene to no avail before Marjorie wouldn't stand for it anymore. She finally woke up from an eight-year-long nightmare. It's as though she got hit over the head with a two-by-four, finally seeing the reality of who she'd married. She did not want her daughter to endure the suffering she'd experienced growing up with her mom. And she sure as hell didn't want Annie to end up in screwed-up relationships later on.

I highly doubt that Marjorie would have ever dumped Craig, let alone ever found her way into a therapist's office, were it not for their having a child. Thankfully, she did seek help, and within a few short months she filed for divorce.

Funny how Marjorie wasn't at all able to see the extent to which she'd sacrificed in the love department by marrying Craig, but she certainly rose to the occasion to protect her own daughter. Thank goodness for Annie! This wasn't easy, though, especially since controlling people tend to get worse when those who once complied with their demands begin to resist them. And Craig was no exception, often threatening and frightening Marjorie. But Marjorie didn't allow him to bully her anymore and she stuck to her guns about leaving. She's well on her way to making a better life for herself. She's chosen to put the whole dating scene on hold for a while, but she'll likely get back in the saddle as she continues to develop a better, more nurturing relationship with herself.

If you find yourself identifying with Katie or Marjorie, again, don't despair. These are really quite common dynamics for women who get involved with chumps. You're in good company. It just may take you a little longer to pull yourself out of the debris.

So now we'll move on to the checklist I use for deciding whether someone is a chump. But keep in mind that everyone will relate differently to the items included. And you might find great variation among your friends or peers in terms of just how chumpy a particular behavior or characteristic might seem. So it's impossible to put them in ascending order since this would simply be my own bias. What I find to be of greatest disturbance might be less obnoxious to you and vice versa. But I have tried to include what I've derived constitutes chumpiness from working with hundreds of women, where at least a handful or more with varying backgrounds and tolerance levels agree. So don't judge your own reaction. Your opinion is no less valid than someone else's.

Also I urge you to take into account the extent to which your guy actually fits these items. In other words, you may be able to answer yes to all items on the list because they've been true at least once in your relationship. But someone who on a rare occasion becomes stubborn and won't apologize for a mistake doesn't really qualify as a chump. We all have a bad day now and again. But if this is a repeated style, then he's more in the ballpark.

I've also tried to steer clear of including specific behaviors as constituting chumpiness, since, again, what might feel like an injury to one gal won't sting at all for another. For instance, if your mate knows that anniversaries and birthdays mean a great deal to you and he consistently blows off these occasions, then you're likely to have a chump on your hands (unless, of course, the week before each of these occasions he's caught you cheating with his best friend). But for some people these celebratory dates don't hold much significance, so it wouldn't be a big deal if they're forgotten.

While I've kept specific behavioral examples out of the criteria list, I do give lots of them while highlighting different stories, because the chump quotient becomes apparent in the context of a real-life scenario.

Onward to the list!

Is Your Guy a Chump?

Please note, before you go any further, that if your guy is abusive in any way he qualifies as a chump no matter what you score on the self-test. Abuse includes any form of verbal, physical, or sexual assault. While all chumps aren't abusers, all abusers are definitely chumps, and of the worst kind. So even if your guy only rates about a 0 or 1 on any of the items below, it doesn't matter. He might be an angel most of the time. But if he's got some switch that gets activated now and again where he feels entitled to hit you or force you to have sex with him when you've said no, for example, then whatever good behavior he demonstrates doesn't wipe out those in the abuse category. If you are in such a situation, please don't close this book thinking I couldn't possibly understand this dynamic. I've been in relationships where I was battered, sexually assaulted, and even had my life threatened. I know every excuse in the book why I deserved what I got. But none of these rationales make any sense. People who abuse others do so because they are weak and unable to deal with frustration. You can never cause someone to behave this way, unless you yourself are being abusive and your mate is operating in self-defense.

Hopefully you're not with an abuser, but if so you need to get whatever help necessary to get yourself to a safe place and out of the relationship. These behaviors should never be tolerated. Now back to the quiz.

If your score doesn't reflect that you're with a chump, remember this is an imperfect test and may not include all indicators. Or even if you discover your guy really isn't that bad, you may still want to get out of the relationship if he's not meeting your needs. Plus you may still have a lot to gain by reading ahead anyway, since it will help you develop better chump radar for future pickings and may help you make sense of previous relationships that didn't work out.

Please use the following scale to rate each item:

0: never   1: rarely   2: sometimes   3: often   4: constantly

Give your mate a 0, 1, 2, 3, or 4 next to each item that best describes him.

Dump That Chump!

__ He doesn't consider my feelings or opinions when making decisions that affect both of us.

__ He lies to me about trivial matters.

__ He lies to me about significant matters.

__ He keeps secrets from me.

__ He devalues me in private (calls me names, makes fun of me, etc.).

__ He ridicules me in front of others.

__ He believes or acts as if his needs are more important than mine rather than treating us as equals.

__ He doesn't make spending time together a priority.

__ Our conversations inevitably end up about him.

__ He stores resentments and then explodes on me.

__ He stores resentments and then passively punishes me. (E.g., he takes a friend to the basketball game even though he'd promised to take you.)

__ He breaks commitments involving both of us without consulting with me or understanding my feelings.

__ He makes promises about the future and doesn't take any actions toward fulfilling them. (E.g., he complains about his job and tells you he's going to look for another one, but never does.)

__ He expects me to pick up after him when we don't have this agreement.

__ He blames me for his mistakes.

__ He doesn't apologize when he's hurt my feelings on something he knew would hurt. (E.g., he promises to take you out to dinner—something he knows you're really looking forward to—and then double-books a business meeting. He goes to the meeting without sharing his concern about how this will affect you or offering any remedy to fix the situation.)

__ He apologizes for hurting my feelings and then turns around and does the same thing knowing I'll be hurt again.

Are You in Love with a Chump?

__ He teases me about things I've told him not to, knowing they're my sensitive spots.

__ He laughs at me at my expense.

__ He tells me things he knows I want to hear, but turns around and does what he wants anyway.

__ He tunes me out when I'm talking to him about important matters.

__ He won't make long-term commitments, and he doesn't give me feedback about why. (E.g., you ask him to come with you to visit your parents and he just says no.)

__ He thinks he's superior to me, disregarding my opinions.

__ He disrespects my family and/or friends.

__ He tries to control my whereabouts (either through manipulation or outright threats of abandonment if I don't comply with his demands).

Add up your points and then use the descriptions below to evaluate your score. Again, please keep in mind that this is a rough guide. This is not rocket science, nor has this quiz been empirically validated. Rather, simply use it as a tool to give you a sense of the kinds of attitudes and styles of relating commonly employed by chumps. While, generally speaking, the higher the score, the greater cause for concern, this isn't a perfect system since all items aren't of equal value, nor will they have the same impact on each person.

For instance, for me personally, if I were with a guy who only occasionally lied to me about important stuff, I would never be able to trust him. Even if I were able to give him a zero on all other items, I'd still think he was a chump and wouldn't be able to have a relationship with him. This is an example of how the lowest possible score might still be grounds for dumping the bum. I just want you to really understand that this is a very subjective rating game, and again it's you who must decide your own tolerance level.

0–5: Virtually chump-free—Generally speaking, if your guy rates a five or less he's probably a pretty good guy, and the few times he behaves badly may not be such a big deal. Hence, he probably deserves to be cut a bit more slack. If you're miserable with him anyway, you may need to take a look at your own issues to see whether unhealed emotional wounds prohibit you from having any tolerance for any errors in a mate's ways. However, if there are other areas of difficulty in the relationship, then he may not warrant any more of your time or energy. He's probably not a chump, but it may be best for you to call it quits with him nonetheless.

Carmine's beau, Paul, had a tendency to blame Carmine for his mistakes, holding her accountable for things that were truly his responsibility. For instance, he'd miss an exit off the freeway and get mad at her because she was talking too much. Or he'd forget to pick up tickets to the concert because she kept him up too late the night before talking about her gossiping coworker. But clearly these were his own misdoings and not her responsibility at all. After all, he's a full-fledged adult who could have easily said, "Please, let's not talk right now so I can focus on the road" or "I have to get some sleep because I have a busy day tomorrow."

In and of themselves these tendencies don't warrant labeling Paul a chump because he would eventually recognize that he was taking his stress out on her and he would apologize. Now, if he weren't able to eventually claim what was his responsibility, then that would be a whole other story. But all of us resort to childlike behaviors now and again under conditions of stress, frustration, or fear. As long as there's some eventual accountability, we need to have some room for these moments and not get too bent out of shape about them.

Blaming others for one's own mistakes is chumpy behavior,

but unless someone does this fairly regularly they don't generally warrant the full label of chump. Concerning this couple, Carmine had many other issues with Paul, having very different visions of their future. He didn't want kids. She did. He's Christian. She's Jewish. Neither could fully embrace the other's religion. He liked lounging in his downtime, whereas she enjoyed being on the move. So in the end, they split up, not because Paul was a chump but because they simply didn't share enough in common for either to be satisfied.

6–20: *Low level*—Guys who fall into this category are what I call "situational chumps." They're not the full-blown chump types, but under stress or when they have a bad day, they're liable to act just like those who manifest the whole enchilada. Most of the time, these guys mean well and do have a sense of remorse when they've acted badly.

If your guy rates at this level, you're probably annoyed with him at times, but he's also got many redeeming qualities that make him lovable. Again, however, if you came up with a score closer to twenty and it's because he received several fours, then the times when he is behaving like a chump may cause enough damage to the relationship and to your self-esteem that it's a good idea to get rid of him. Or, it's also quite possible that with the help of couples counseling you both might be able to make significant changes in how you relate to each other. In fact, if you were to take the quiz again answering about your *own* behavior, your rating would land in this range as well.

Alexa and Bob were dating for about two years before coming to see me. They were a delightful couple, with Alexa a bundle of energy and Bob, though a bit more subdued, articulate and quite engaging. When they were getting along well, they both felt they would have a wonderful future together. But one of them would inevitably get tweaked by the other's behavior, and they would rapidly spiral into a dark hole of despair.

As it turned out, both Alexa and Bob had experienced fairly emotionally abusive childhoods with parents who failed to supply many fundamental needs. They were both hungry for someone to provide the emotional nurturance that was lacking in their youth. So when one or the other became distant or preoccupied with something, the other would feel wounded. Because neither of them had learned healthy ways to manage disappointment or frustration, they would lash out at each other and behave more like two three-year-olds in the throes of a temper tantrum than like the two intelligent adults they were. Fortunately with some new tools and new insights they were able to mend their relationship. But it's important to understand that *both* Alexa and Bob were willing to do the emotional work necessary to make changes in their behavior toward each other.

Jane and Ian did not share this resolve. Jane had dragged Ian's butt into therapy, threatening to leave him if he didn't stop making fun of her (even though he was "just teasing"), leaving his crud all over their place, and blaming her for everything that went wrong in their relationship. Unlike Bob, however, Ian had no interest in making any of these changes. He just wanted her to stop whining already and have more sex with him. It became quite obvious early in their counseling that he had no interest in understanding his part in why their relationship was deteriorating rapidly. He bailed out of counseling after a few sessions. And she ultimately decided it was best to move on.

So if your mate rates at this level, ask yourself whether he is truly willing to work on his issues or whether he's pretty much blown you off whenever you've tried to tell him what hurts or bothers you. If he's made promises to change but hasn't, it may mean that he truly wants to, but doesn't know how. If that's the case, then offer to seek counseling with him. But if he refuses to do his part, then regardless of how low he rates on this scale, you're probably better off ending the relationship before you get in even deeper.

21–50: *Moderate level*—With this kind of guy, you're probably upset with him a good chunk of the time. To receive this kind of score he's doing either a little bit of all these things or several of them a lot. So no matter how you look at it, you've definitely got a chump on your hands. But whether the relationship is salvageable or not will depend primarily on his willingness to change (which isn't very likely) and, secondarily, on your own personal love goals.

I think you could do much better. But I don't know your particular situation. You may have a great deal invested in the relationship, including kids and financial dependency. Or maybe the times that are good are excellent and you can make peace with the rest that don't work so well. But if this is the case, you'll have to find a way to accept and not be so affected by his chumpy behavior and seriously lower your expectations of him changing. This is not a bad choice, but I do advise that you thoroughly consider the ramifications to your happiness in life. If nothing else, do seek the aid of a counselor to help you figure out what's the best course of action.

If, on the other hand, you're unmarried, have little time invested, and no kids or financial dependency, and you've just been waiting for his full potential to emerge, then I highly recommend you carry on with the plan to dump your chump. And don't continue to give power to your fears. You can and will heal through whatever scares you about moving on. And someday you'll be able to look back at this relationship and laugh about it.

51–75: *High level*—A guy who falls into this category doesn't stand a very good chance of ever having a gratifying intimate relationship with anyone. Because, no matter how you spin it, you're rating your guy pretty high on many of these items. And none of these characteristics are anything to be proud of.

If you find yourself making justifications for your guy as to why he rates this way, stop for a moment. Go back and review these again, and think of how you'd feel if your best friend described her guy this way. My guess is you would worry about her well-being and encourage her to rethink her choice. This is not a pretty picture, and isn't likely to change—no matter how much you invest in the relationship. This is well beyond situational chumpiness.

If you don't dump this guy, you would be seriously depriving yourself of a happy future. Again, I don't know the specifics of your situation. But no matter how intertwined your life is with him and how difficult it might be to set yourself free, you should seriously consider moving on. If you don't, you are underestimating your value by taking a lot of crap from someone who doesn't respect you. No matter what level of self-worth you started with, even if it was low, you're only making it worse by staying in this type of relationship. Your self-esteem can't possibly improve in this kind of relationship, no matter what changes you make personally. In fact, your sense of value is most likely at an all-time low and you don't recognize that you have options. So I strongly encourage you to make a commitment to better your life and take the plunge back into single life.

76–100: *Red alert! Toxicity level*—Get out! This is serious business here. No matter what this guy's excuse is (he was dropped on his head at birth; his mother beat him to a pulp daily; his father abandoned him and his seven siblings, leaving them hungry with a disabled mother), it doesn't matter. He's bad news and even if he has had a horrific history that has led him to hold on to highly maladaptive relationship patterns, he's gotta go. You can't be his therapist, and you can't fix him. This is the type of guy who has no self-awareness and is going to continually hurt you. If he does by chance make efforts to seriously change and heal whatever has caused him to be such a chump, you can always get back with him (though you'd have to seriously consider why you'd want to). Of course, be careful that you haven't stacked the deck in your favor by giving him a higher rating than he truly warrants. You're allowed to leave him no matter what!

Though again this is not an objective rating system or psychological profiling tool, there is a good chance you're involved with someone far worse than a chump—very likely someone with Narcissistic Personality Disorder and/or Antisocial Personality Disorder (also known as a sociopath or psychopath). These types do not tend to change, and even when they do seek help, it's usually because they want advice on how to fix someone else or they've been forced into treatment because of having broken a law of some sort. They do not take any responsibility for their own actions or see the impact of their behavior on others. They lack empathy, and without empathy one cannot have a successful intimate relationship. So if this is your situation, please run for the hills now!

Varying Breeds of Chumps

No two chumps are exactly alike. And if you've had more than one relationship with a chump you may have a hard time identifying another chump, since you might expect all chumps to come in the same uniform package. But chumps come in as many varieties as automobiles or cereals. Though the varieties are endless, there seem to be some clusters lending themselves to five general categories: the snake, the grizzly bear, the weasel, the pig, and the sloth.

Of course, in reviewing these, please keep in mind that these are imperfect groupings. They won't cover every type of chump and no guy will fit neatly into only one category. You're bound to see overlap with the others. That's okay. You won't benefit any more by finding the precise description—and no insurance company or judge will award you extra in punitive damages because you isolated the exact diagnosis of your chump. But ideally these descriptions will help you understand that while your chump may seem like he's in a class all by himself (and therefore no one can understand your plight), he's probably more like others than meets the eye. Again, if you get away from focusing on specific behaviors, you'll be more likely to see a certain type of process that qualifies your guy as a chump.

The Snake: The snakelike chump slithers in and out of everything. One minute he's hiding, curled up, looking harmless. The next minute he's wrapped around you, either squeezing the life out of you or biting you with venomous fangs. He's extremely difficult to pin down, manipulating his way out of everything. He's the type who can make you feel crazy, convincing others and you that whatever you saw was in your imagination. He may lie, cheat, or steal—anything to get out of being responsible for his behavior. He may look beautiful on the outside, but he's not so on the inside. You're his prey and he's out to get fed.

Sonya's boyfriend, Trevor, completely personified the snake-type chump. He constantly passed the buck to her, always coming up with an excuse why he shouldn't be held accountable for his actions. He, like many snake-types, had multiple women on the side—just in case he got tired of Sonya. When she would express jealousy in response to his blatant flirting with other women, he would tell her she was too possessive and no guy would ever put up with her if she couldn't handle her guy simply being "friendly." I'd hardly call grabbing other women's asses friendly behavior!

Because Sonya was so used to being put down for her needs (that's right, some unhealed childhood bruises at play), she rarely questioned Trevor's explanations for his behavior. Rather, she would automatically take his input at face value and conclude that she was being irrational. All the while, though, she'd feel really bad inside and unworthy of better treatment.

Fortunately for Sonya, she'd had a few relationships with guys who had been nice to her. Though she hadn't been particularly attracted to them she was able to recognize that good guys don't treat their girlfriends as though they don't matter. And she decided she better get rid of Trevor before she lost her sanity altogether.

Mind you, all snake-types aren't so toxic. Just like in the real snake world, there are garden snakes as well as rattlers and boas. But even with the milder garden-variety snakes, there ain't gonna be a whole lot of lovin' comin' your way. If you have needs for affection and kindness (as I believe all humans have), you're going to remain pretty thirsty if you settle for a snakelike guy, even if he's not a really big chump. These types lack empathy, and they don't make good mates.

The Grizzly Bear: The grizzly bear often appears to offer strength and protection, qualities that can be very appealing, especially to a woman who's seeking a guy to "take care of her." But when he's not offering snuggly hugs and keeping you from harm, he can be extremely domineering and even threatening. He growls a lot, baring his very sharp teeth. He takes what he wants—when he wants it—with little regard for the trail of destruction he leaves behind. From a distance he may appear warm and fuzzy, but beware when his needs aren't being met right away. He'll do whatever it takes to get his fill.

Contrary to cartoon images of a grizzly, the real-life version is not usually very warm and fuzzy. He may appear sweet and cuddly while sleeping or fully satiated, but more often he's a tyrant and a bully, demanding attention and servitude. If he's displeased, he lets you know way more forcefully than necessary. He may not ever cross the line into actual abusive behavior, but it's very hard to feel safe in his company. His offer of protection often comes with a very high price—like the loss of your freedom.

The Weasel: The weasel appears playful and cute. But don't be fooled—he can be very sneaky, just like the snake. But while we are generally leery of the snake, the weasel can catch you by surprise. The weasel lulls you into a false sense of security, while he's actually up to no good. Weasels make lots of false promises just to get you hooked. When they fail to keep their promises, they often make up an even bigger story.

Rhonda met Mike while she was playing tennis with one of her girlfriends. Mike approached Rhonda with tennis racket in hand and a huge smile. He told her he liked her game, and he invited her to play sometime. They started dating and found they had a great deal in common—both were quite athletic and eager to enjoy life. What wasn't initially apparent, however, was that Mike was basically a con artist. He acted like he was a rich guy, when in fact he only had a part-time job and basically mooched off his friends. After a couple of months Rhonda found herself paying for all of their dates, buying into his excuses such as:

"Oops, I left my wallet at home," or "I don't know what's wrong with my credit. Hope you don't mind paying, sweetie. I'll get you back later." Later would never come. Meanwhile her bank account was dwindling fast, accommodating his champagne tastes on her beer budget.

The Pig: The name pretty much says it all. And I don't mean that really cute, petlike pig. Rather, I'm referring to the stereotypical image of the true slob. This guy leaves a trail of crap wherever he goes. Not just piles of laundry, dirty dishes, and unidentifiable green stuff in the fridge but emotional messes as well. Basically, he doesn't care who he offends—he just goes for whatever he wants regardless of the consequences. He may tell racist and sexist jokes, without caring if he hurts anyone's feelings in the process.

No matter how much you beg and plead with this guy to pick up after himself and use some manners, he doesn't change. He is who he is, and he expects you to live with it. But you know what? Screw him (no, not literally)! You don't have to put up with this guy. You can leave his sorry ass. Granted all of us can be a bit messy now and again, and you yourself might suffer from disorganization problems, but if so you probably recognize you need improvement and would certainly not expect others to pick up after you. The pig doesn't take any responsibility for his actions.

I know many people who thought they could get around the pig problem by hiring a full-time maid. But no maid can clean up the emotional slop he creates. So be careful if this is the solution you're contemplating. You may be better off just dumping him!

The Sloth: A friend of mine went to Costa Rica and observed a sloth. She reported that the sloth basically stays in one place all the time and comes down from the tree once a week to defecate. (I know, not a nice image.) The human sloth is quite similar. This kind of chump doesn't abuse you or actively make you feel bad about yourself like some of the other types. But he can be just as toxic.

This type often passively agrees to things but never follows up. He expects forgiveness simply because he'll convince you that he had good intentions but he just forgot. But hey—after a while intentions don't matter if you can never rely on the guy to make good on his promises and agreements. So if you're with this kind of guy, don't be fooled into believing that someday he'll become reliable Mr. Go-Getter or you'll be holding your breath for a long time. He might even be the nicest guy in the world, but you're not going to get your needs met if you actually want an intimate partner.

Now take a moment to determine which category best describes your chump. Having a visual will help give you more strength when you make the break. But if the images I've used don't work for you, please create your own. You can come up with other animals or anything else that puts him in perspective. Maybe bugs: cockroaches, stink bugs, ants, or wasps? Maybe marine life: sharks, eels, jellyfish, or lobsters? Or maybe types of cars? It doesn't matter what you pick. Just pick something that adequately conjures up the chumplike essence of your man.

Hopefully this chapter has shed some light on the degree to which your mate is a chump. And even if you discovered your chump isn't so toxic, that doesn't mean you should hang on to him. In the next chapter, I give you a brief overview of what to expect over the next several weeks, and then you'll be ready to take the plunge and dump that chump.

Chapter 4

Dr. Debra's Nine-Step Success Plan

$\mathcal{I}$'ve set this book up as a nine-step plan, with no particular time frame. Getting through each step may take you a couple of days or a couple of weeks. There's no correct pace—it's up to you. Many situations might complicate matters, causing you to need either extra time to dump your chump or even more time to make room for Mr. Right. So please don't pressure yourself to go faster than you're able.

For instance, if you've got kids, then obviously their needs must be taken into account before dumping your chump, especially if your chump decides to fight you for custody (even though he was more akin to a sperm donor than a real dad). Or, maybe you don't have children, but you share property. Any time you've intertwined finances with a mate, such as owning a house together, you're likely to require continued contact while in the process of dividing things up. It wouldn't necessarily be wise to just walk away. Thus, if any scenarios like these apply to you,

you're probably going to have to come head to head with this guy following a breakup. And, clearly, such contact won't be easy and understandably may delay your progress.

Whatever it takes, however, don't judge yourself. If you find yourself getting stuck, be proactive and get the help you need. Don't use circumstances as excuses. At the very least, make a commitment to work toward your goal.

Once you are finally ready to take the plunge, follow the tips ahead to keep you moving on a positive track. And should you experience any bumps or detours along the way, just get right back onto your path as quickly as possible. Slipups are to be expected, even in the simplest of situations. Trust me. I know this firsthand!

I had a relationship during most of my twenties that has served as a big inspiration for writing this book. I often think back to that time in my life and wish I had had someone steering me away from that dead-end road. Unfortunately it took me almost seven years to finally end the agony I endured by being in love with that chump. And for a long time I lived in total regret and resentment for having stayed and wasted so much time. In my mind, I blamed him for holding me hostage, when in fact all the while I had the power to leave. I was just too weak and too scared to assert this option!

But, today, I can honestly say I have no regrets. Once I got over blaming the chump for my choices and getting rid of my shame about being in a bad relationship, I was finally able to cut myself slack. I realized I wasn't able to do it any other way. Had I had different tools and better resources, I might have been able to leave much sooner. But I didn't, so beating myself up or living in regret did me no good—that's what really wasted my time. Instead, I learned how to be compassionate for my process and chalk up those years to a necessary chapter in my life. I learned a great deal, especially about what kind of relationship I didn't want to have.

I loved this guy (we'll call him Pete) with every cell of my body. We had incredible chemistry. My heart skipped a beat each time I saw him. The first few months of our dating were especially incredible. He appeared as totally into me as I was into him. He couldn't do enough to please me.

We met while we were both in college. Believe it or not, we locked eyes while he was using a pay phone on campus. I think Cupid had a leftover dose of love potion in his arrow that hadn't been fully injected in his previous prey, and we got more than the necessary dosage. We couldn't get enough of each other. He told me numerous times I was the one for him and that we would build a happy life together.

But things didn't stay rosy for very long. Within a few months, Pete began to show his true colors, bearing no resemblance to any rainbow I'd ever seen. Sure, he was still as smooth as silk, charming the pants off me anytime I had any criticism of him. But it was clear that the writing was on the wall: THIS RELATIONSHIP IS DOOMED. Of course, even if you'd given me 250 percent magnifying power, I still would not have seen it.

In hindsight, I'd say that after about three months, I was completely hooked, and I wholeheartedly believed there would never be anyone better for me. He could have been a serial killer and I'd have found some way to justify his behavior. Tragically, I truly believed I couldn't and shouldn't live without him. Thankfully, he wasn't a serial killer and I never had to test this hypothesis, but you get the picture.

Though he'd initially been quite responsive to my assertiveness, he soon began responding to my proactive approach to him as being smothering. It seemed like one minute he was madly in love with me and the next minute he couldn't get away from me fast enough. And progressively he spent more time with his friends and much less time with me. Late-night poker games and trips to Europe with his buddies became far more appealing than snuggling with me.

No wonder over time I grew more and more insecure, as though I hadn't already had enough of that insecure bug before I'd met him. And as my insecurities heightened, so too did his rejecting behaviors. We must have broken up at least twenty times over the course of our relationship, and each time I'd beg for his return. (Well, a couple of times he came running back, but I had wrongly assumed this was because he'd actually matured and regretted the loss. As it turned out, he came back because of ulterior motives, like needing a free place to park his butt.) At one point, he'd lost his job and "needed" me. I couldn't have been happier. "Now he would never leave me after all the nurturing I'd given him," I thought. Wrong!

I don't need to give you too many of the gory details, but suffice it to say that in the end nothing had changed after each reunion. He'd even promised marriage to me on several occasions—without any intention of ever following through. The bottom line was that he wanted a loyal and committed girlfriend, but he clearly didn't hold himself to the same standard of accountability.

Thank god I finally came to my senses and made the final break. But, boy, that probably ranked as one of the most painful things I'd ever had to do. It required me to lead with my brain, with my heart kicking and screaming along the way. Leaving someone I was still madly in love with was an alien concept. I'd been taught that love conquers all and I should stick with someone through thick and thin. I'd never read the fine print that said, "Exception: These rules don't apply when dealing with a chump. When that's the case, you should run for the hills despite how much love your heart feels." Fortunately, I did ultimately take the plunge back into singlehood. And before too long my broken heart mended, and I preserved my sanity.

Breaking Up Is Hard to Do—But It Is Doable

There's an old song written by Neil Sedaka called "Breaking Up Is Hard to Do." And nothing could be more on track, if you have any heart at all. Of course, chumps break hearts all the time, often thoughtlessly and without ever looking back. But if you have feelings for someone and you've invested time and energy in building a relationship, it's never going to be easy just to walk away. And even if you've just been attached to a dream of what could have been, without a whole lot of reality backing up the illusion, it's still going to feel like a loss, no matter what.

Breaking up with a chump can be the hardest of all because the attachment is so intense and the fear around the loss is equally as brutal. Also, more often than not, your self-esteem is in the toilet and you have grown to fear being alone. He's probably told you things like "You'd be nothin' without me" or "You'll never find anyone better." Worse yet, he may have brainwashed you to believe that he couldn't live without you and that because he's given so much to you, you're now under permanent obligation to stay with him.

Victoria was finally ready to make the break from Tom, a weasel type with a little grizzly bear rising. After two years of intense fighting, catching him in lies and never getting a straight answer to a question, Victoria couldn't take the pain and agony anymore. She'd tried on numerous occasions to end the relationship, but always during a fight. And when the anger wore off, he would convince her that she'd be making a big mistake by walking out. Before you know it, she'd be the one apologizing to him for getting him so upset. Ultimately she'd feel like a bitch for even thinking of leaving him. He would manipulate her into believing that he was doing her a favor by taking her back in.

This cycle just about sent her to the loony bin. But thankfully she had enough sanity left to recognize that if she were to spend the rest of her life with this guy, there wouldn't be much left of it. Either she'd end up killing herself or shoving him in front of a large truck (not really, but suicidal and homicidal thoughts were definitely coming more into her focus). She tried many times to finally cut it off with Tom without succeeding. But after getting wind of the tips and tools outlined in this book, she ultimately succeeded.

Despite how hard it might be to break up with a chump, think about how hard it is to stay with one. It can't be easy. Remember all those sleepless nights, turning to chocolate for comfort because he was nowhere to be found? Remember calling friends at all hours of the night sobbing about what an ass he is or believing you're no longer lovable? Or what about those lonely nights when he was either out with his buddies until the wee hours or fixated on the tube, ignoring all your attempts to be affectionate?

I'm not trying to make you feel bad. I just want you to really be aware of what you've endured. I'm sure you can tolerate the breakup. Besides, being in a chronic state of despair causes a great deal of stress. And this is terribly hard on the body. So believe me, whatever pain you're trying to avoid by not making the break isn't saving you from anything. And it's only going to get worse. So you might as well dive in sooner rather than later. I assure you that you can handle it, and it won't be as bad as you fear if you diligently apply and practice the tips ahead.

Eliminating Shame

Before moving on to the actual methods for dumping a chump, it's important to rid yourself of any shame you carry for being with your guy. So first let's do a quick assessment of how bad you've been bitten by the shame bug.

For the following items give yourself a 0, 1, 2, 3, or 4 with each meaning:

0: never 1: rarely 2: sometimes 3: often 4: constantly

___ I don't like myself.

___ I think there's something wrong with me.

___ I believe I'm unlovable.

___ I believe I'm damaged goods.

___ I believe no one else will ever want me.

___ I isolate from my friends and family because I'm embarrassed about being in this relationship.

___ I'm afraid to tell people how bad I feel about myself.

___ I lie about my relationship, making it sound better than it is.

___ I believe I've ruined my life.

___ I engage in using substances (e.g., drugs, alcohol, food) or some behavior (e.g., shopping, gambling, working) in excess to numb myself from feeling bad.

Now add up your score and see where you fall on the shame scale.

0–10: This score implies only minor traces of shame. At this level, you may only notice shame when you're faced with extreme circumstances—like excess stress at work causing you to fear failure, or when you've been in a prolonged toxic relationship like the one you're in with your chump. So rest assured. You're not too bad off. And you are likely to have an easier time doing the dirty deed and moving on with your life. I'm not saying it will be a walk in the park, but at least you don't have the added burden of attacking the core of yourself in the process.

11–20: This score implies that you do experience shame at times regardless of what's going on in your life. You might be doing great and still have some feelings of not being good enough. You may have become good at camouflaging your shame, so you may not even notice when it's there. But your score indicates that you're not as strong in your self-worth as you need to be to be able to have a healthy intimate relationship. And you may need to do some prep work before taking the final plunge. I think with some positive affirmations and a commitment to be nice to yourself, you won't trip yourself up too much. But do be aware of a tendency to get down on yourself, and don't give your shaming voice the power to make you feel bad. Stand up to it instead. These are irrational thoughts that have most likely escalated or have been the direct result of being in a relationship with a chump. The sooner you leave, the sooner you'll be on the road to ridding yourself of any traces of shame.

21–30: At this level, you've most likely already identified yourself as a shame-based person. You may have even done some therapy work already, knowing that you don't feel good about yourself. Though it's possible that you once felt great and now, as a result of being with your chump, you're scoring high, I venture a guess that you had some self-worth issues long before you ever met your chump. And you may have a history of hooking up with guys who treat you badly. You've got to put down the hammer and stop banging yourself on the head.

Chances are, you're far too hard on yourself. And how you behave toward yourself most likely mimics how your chump treats you. Don't worry! You're not at all doomed. You just need to recognize that you are making the process more painful than it has to be. So you need to be extra concerned with recognizing these demeaning voices you carry in your head and telling them to go away. You may have to practice a bit of the "fake it 'til you make it" philosophy. That is, you'll need to act as if you're worthy before you actually believe it. But before too long, your actions and beliefs will be in sync. Plus, you need to be especially diligent in practicing self-soothing and self-acceptance. Otherwise, if you wait until you truly feel good about yourself before you make the break, you'll be creating a recipe for more self-hatred rather than moving toward self-love. So take action to find and use whatever resources you need in addition to this self-help book so you can begin giving yourself the gift of self-love.

31–40: If you scored in this range, you probably feel buried in self-disgust most of the time. And my heart bleeds for you. I wouldn't be surprised if you're someone who had been abused or neglected in childhood and/or who got involved early on in relationships with people who mistreated you. You may be so familiar with being in a shame state that you don't even have anything to contrast it with. But it's time you break free from such self-abuse and learn the art of self-love. (You'll get lots of help with this in Chapter Nine!)

Whatever you do, don't shame yourself with this information. Don't think of yourself as a freak. You're not alone. I've worked with many women who have a lot going on for themselves but who feel as if they are worthless. Believe me, I know how you feel. I, myself, lived a huge chunk of my life in this state of self-hatred. Not a good place to be whether you're single, with the greatest guy on earth, or with a chump. But if you want to thrive and have a loving, nurturing relationship someday, you simply must commit to healing your shame.

At this level, it's probably mandatory to seek outside help, either individual or group psychotherapy and/or some other resource focused on eliminating shame and improving your self-worth. You probably don't believe me, but you ARE worthy of love. You're NOT damaged, and you CAN have a happy life! Don't skimp on self-care! Take action now! You may even skip or take a detour from the sequence of the book and move ahead to Chapter Nine—then you can come back.

Regardless of your level, if you're prone to any unnecessary shame, make a commitment right now to get rid of it. Otherwise as you're trying to go through this process you will likely fall into what I call a "shame hole." Once in a shame hole, the room gets very dark, and it's virtually impossible to see solutions, let alone take any action. So you must work toward spotting your shame holes and filling them up every day—for as long as it takes until you finally learn to THRIVE.

Sure, some amount of shame is part of the human experience and keeps us humble and acting kindly toward others. But more often than not, people who have attached themselves to a chump carry far more shame than is warranted. If you let shame guide you, you'll remain stuck feeling bad about yourself. You are not a bad person for being in this situation, and you certainly don't deserve to be treated badly!

The good news is that simply recognizing that you're prone to shame is half the battle. And with this acknowledgment and the commitment to rid yourself of toxic shame residue, you can proceed with your breakup plan. But if at any time along the way you get stuck in a shame hole, please practice the following exercise (and seek extra help if necessary).

Shame-Hole Filler: Whenever you start to feel the hammer pounding on your self-esteem, please repeat aloud the following:

"I know I'm prone to beating myself up and making myself the enemy/bad one. But I need to break this pattern and stop being a magnet for mistreatment. I deserve better than what I've allowed myself to experience, and it's my job to give myself the love and nurturance I need to feel good about myself. I can make my life better, and I don't need anyone else to do it for me or to give me permission."

What Lies Ahead

Okay, you're ready to move forward. In the chapters ahead you will learn many tools and methods for actually making the break and then how to move through the pain quickly. I will show you how to quit pining for, romanticizing, and fantasizing about your chump and how to move from feelings of anger and hurt to contentment. Of great importance is the chapter on self-soothing, particularly if you've recognized that you tend to fall into shame holes. So most definitely pay attention to these resources.

Commonly, breakups with chumps yield feelings of regret and a strong desire to blame the guy. But staying angry at him and failing to own your own choices will only set you up to be a target for another chump. Instead, you need to accept your own responsibility to create a fulfilling love life. You must come to understand what brought you to this guy to begin with, identify the red flags you missed, and uncover any unresolved childhood issues that interfere with your ability to select a healthy mate.

After the grunt work, it's time to party. You're going to be the birthday girl, regardless of the fact that it probably won't be your actual birthday when you enter this phase. No matter. You will lavish in a full-blown celebration of YOU! And last but not least you'll dive back into the dating world feeling sexy and alive. But no sex! (This is critical, and you'll see why later.) And this time around you will have your heart and your head in sync.

Onward!

Chapter 5

Dump That Chump

$\mathcal{E}$ven in healthy relationships, people sometimes decide to part ways. These partings occur for a variety of reasons having nothing to do with anyone's bad behavior. For instance, take a couple who haven't been together all that long, and one gets a job in another state. They love and respect each other, but they'd rather not attempt a long-distance relationship because they both feel it would be too stifling. So they sadly say good-bye. Or think of the couple who've been involved for quite a while but who have very different long-term goals—e.g., one wants children, while the other wants to explore the globe unencumbered by those adorable little brats. (Mind you, I adore children. But they sure can be a handful, and if someone doesn't want the challenge, it's far better not to have any.) Or there's the common couple who come to realize they have very low compatibility, and they find themselves drifting apart.

Often in these types of scenarios, the breakups are mutually decided, and they come about by a natural course. Usually both people are mature enough to see that letting go is a better choice than hanging on. Although it is a painful process, they're not bitter. No one feels betrayed, taken advantage of, or misinformed. These relationships warrant a respectful breakup process, with each person given ample time to express feelings and regrets, and to support each other while disconnecting. A friendship may be highly possible once they've each grieved the loss. Nothing less than a face-to-face, caring, and comforting dialogue is in order.

But, hey, the breakup protocol or prescription when you're dealing with a chump can be tossed right out the window. With these breakups whatever gets you out is okay, barring shooting him in the head or running his car into a ditch. (Though these ideas might be appealing, don't act on them, of course!☺) In case you're resistant to the idea that you don't have to go out of your way to have a "nice" breakup, ask yourself: Has your chump been playing fair up until now? I seriously doubt it, so there's no reason for you to have to go the extra mile as you should for someone who's been a good mate. Of course, if you're able to maintain your own integrity and go about the process with dignity, then fine. But please don't hold yourself to any strict criteria. Chumps don't play by healthy rules, so you don't have to hold yourself to an unrealistic standard when doing the dirty job.

Below are several acceptable methods to dump your chump. Feel free to modify these in any way you wish. Just make sure you don't get caught up in some perfectionist trap that keeps you stuck. In other words, there's no best way to dump a chump. Even if you do a lousy job, as long as you're out, that's all that matters. Set your standards low, and then you won't disappoint yourself or have anything to feel guilty about. However, in implementing any of these strategies, keep in mind the following:

✦ Avoid initiating a breakup during an argument. It's better to have a time-out first. Clear your head and approach from a position of strength and a sound mind.

✦ If at all possible, avoid breaking up during a time of acute crisis. For instance, if you just received news that you've been fired from your job, or that your favorite aunt has been diagnosed with a terminal illness, wait a week or so. Of course, keep this in perspective. If you tend to be a bit of a drama queen or tend to experience every little upset as a crisis, make sure you don't keep finding external life events reasons to prolong the inevitable breakup.

✦ Make sure you have set in place an immediate backup support plan. Before taking the plunge, check in with your best friend, sister, parent—whomever you find to be a comforting person or group. Find out his/her availability over the next couple of weeks. Go down your list of people and alert these folks of your potential need for their extra support. Should your strength start to falter, which may very well happen, you'll be grateful that you already have this in place.

✦ Have a prewritten journal entry reminding you of why you're going through with this breakup. List as extensively as possible all the reasons for letting go: he treats you badly, you generally feel miserable in the relationship, you don't like yourself anymore and that's a horrible way to live, etc. Keep this close at hand at all times. Make extra copies to keep with you at work, in the car, and at home.

Methods to Dump Your Chump

I've outlined three methods to dump your chump: the classic "Dear John" letter, the Bye-Bye Talk, and the Houdini. The method you choose will be up to you. You might even use a combo pack of all three in some variation. If you have a better method, by all means go for it. I have no ego invested in you using one of my suggestions. (But please do e-mail me with your creative ideas, as I may be able to use them for future editions of this book!)

The classic "Dear John" letter. While this is a completely tacky option if you were ending a relationship with a good guy, it's perfectly acceptable with a chump, particularly if you've already experienced one or more unsuccessful attempts at setting yourself free. The key to a positive outcome with the letter method is to make sure you write it in such a way as to leave no doors open for arguments. You must be crystal clear that it's over (even if you're incredibly ambivalent) and you must make it about you, not about what he's done to force you into this position. Otherwise you leave room for him once again to seduce you into believing you're the one at fault, or convince you why he's the best guy for you.

The "Dear John" letter is a good-bye letter. It's not an opportunity to express your feelings of sadness and hurt, nor is it a time to air your differences. You've already had countless late-night conversations and crying spells trying to get him to understand how lonely and disappointed you have been with him. He hasn't listened to you up until now. Or if he's heard you, he certainly hasn't responded with any meaningful behavioral changes—or you wouldn't be in this position. And I highly doubt that he's ever going to "get it."

The letter method is also not the time for name-calling or giving the laundry list of how he's failed you. If you point out all the things he's done to you he's going to have an opening to argue with you. For instance, if you name all his offenses (e.g., he makes promises he never keeps or he spends too much time with the guys), he's just going to justify his behavior. And he might even blame you. God knows, you don't need anything else attacking your self-esteem. So definitely don't engage in pointing out his flaws. If anything, state the reason why you're leaving him as something about you—e.g., "I'm not able to handle our differences" or "I can't handle all the pain I feel in this relationship."

Here's an example of a good "Dear John" letter:

Dear [his name here],

I'm so sorry to tell you in this way, but I am ending our relationship. As much as I've hoped we could work things out, I no longer hold that hope. I'm not happy with us and I don't believe we will ever have a chance. I want a different relationship than I have with you. I don't want to hear any excuses or bargaining pleas. I don't like how you treat me and I'm moving on. I truly wish you all the best. I request that you please refrain from calling/e-mailing me for the next month. I'll be in touch in a few weeks [you can actually name a date here] and if there is any business for us to attend to, we can make arrangements at that time.

Sincerely, [your name]

I know. The part about wishing him the best might actually sound repulsive to you right now, since you may even be wishing him dead. But go ahead, bite the bullet, and wish him well even though you may not mean it right now. Eventually this statement will be true, once you've fully let go and gotten rid of your resentment.

If you don't have any external ties with the guy, then you can leave out the whole second half. Just end with "I request that you refrain from contacting me." Period. End of story. You may think this is harsh, but trust me: it's really just clear and to the point. Anything else gives him room to manipulate you, which, by the way, he may try to do anyway. He might disregard your boundary and contact you. He may call you a "bitch" or worse yet, a "cunt." But you must refrain from responding. Your only responsibility is to send the letter. You do not need to reply to anything he has to say in return. And quite frankly, I recommend that if he contacts you, you just tear up his communications, or press that wonderful button called "delete," before even reading what he has to say. And if he calls, don't answer, and don't listen to the messages.

No matter what the temptation, avoid all pet names and terms of endearment. And stay away from name-calling or pointing the finger at him, hoping this one time he'll be a man and cop to his responsibility in the demise of your relationship. If anything, this will just cause him to be defensive and be eager to give you a piece of his mind. And you definitely don't need his pieces!

Be especially careful not to get caught up in wanting to make it all right for him. Regardless of the fact that your guy is a chump, he may actually feel bad. He may even express regret or remorse for his behavior—though he'll probably never admit this to you. But if he's really going to change you can always get back in touch with him in six months to a year and do an assessment then. At this point, if he were to make any promises, they would all qualify as lip service. I'm sure you've pointed out to him hundreds of times already the things he says and does that repeatedly cause you unhappiness. So don't nurture him through this. He'll find his own sources of repair, and if he doesn't, it's still not your responsibility. Plus that would be even more evidence that he was never really serious.

If you and your chump have intertwined lives in a significant way, then obviously this process won't be this simple. You may need to add a sentence or two, highlighting ways the two of you can exchange your things or handle business matters. For instance you might add, "I know you have things at my home, and I have stuff at yours. Please pick a window of time where you can drop off my stuff in a box on the side porch." The idea here is to avoid any face-to-face contact. If you have to see him in person, then have a friend or other support person by your side.

Whatever you do, don't get caught up in needing contact with him because he has a few trivial items of yours. For instance, if you left behind your favorite pair of panties in his dresser drawer, you can buy yourself another pair, even if this sets you back a bit financially. Don't use financial excuses to override your emotional well-being.

Certainly if you have left behind meaningful or irreplaceable items like your grandmother's wedding ring or very expensive things like several pairs of Prada shoes, then you may need to do a bit of negotiating to reclaim your stuff. I suggest the one-year rule: If in one year from now you think you'd still regret having left these items behind, then make efforts to retrieve them. Anything that would go in the trash or to the Goodwill within the next six months to a year doesn't need reclaiming. You can live without it.

Justine had a miserable time reclaiming her stuff from Steven. After spending a whole year together you'd think Steven would have demonstrated some class by giving Justine back her things. But nooooo! She'd given him his walking papers through a letter, and she requested that he contact her to exchange their belongings. She gave him several times when she would be available, and he continued to ignore her. After weighing the costs to her to keep running after him, she opted to walk away and cut her losses. This took quite a bit of coaxing, but once she realized that she was actually trying to maintain contact with him and that this was doing her no good, the material items seemed far less important.

The Bye-Bye Talk: This method is virtually the same as the "Dear John" letter but it's done verbally either on the phone or in person. One major benefit to doing this method in person is that you have the opportunity to take your important stuff right on the spot by having the meeting at his place.

The key is to make it short and to the point. This is trickier than the letter because chances are he's going to want to either talk you out of it or make you feel like you're an idiot. Or he may twist it around to seem like he's actually breaking up with you. No matter. Let him think whatever he wants. His thoughts about you don't have to mean anything to you.

You must be strong and not give him power over your feelings. Even if he does manage to get in a few digs, keep a strong boundary and go through with the actions anyway. Believe it or not, you can feel bad and still act on behalf of your own best interests. You've made this decision to dump him for good reason.

If he does turn on the charm, keep in mind that he is manipulating you. He's not being sincere. Even if he really feels bad, there's no reason to believe that he will follow through on any promises of behavioral change. He would only be talking out of a sense of loss, and the minute he thinks he's rehooked you, he'll be up to his old shenanigans again.

Be strong, girl! You will get through this. And you will feel better. I would rather you stick to the letter method if you don't think you can handle his commentary. But I know there are often many circumstances that would make a face-to-face breakup necessary. Just make sure you're not convincing yourself that you have to talk to him again because you want his validation. Don't go to an empty well for water. He doesn't give you what you need! You're thirsty—go get a drink somewhere else.

The Houdini: With this method, you simply stop all contact with no explanation or information. Obviously your ability to simply end ties with no communication is only workable if you have nothing intertwined (or nothing you couldn't live without), there would be no detrimental consequences, and your guy scores quite high on the chump scale. Or if these conditions have mostly been met and you've also repeatedly attempted to break up, only to have him disregard you, then this may also be the method of choice.

An extra cautionary note: If your chump has shown any signs of stalking or obsessive-compulsive behavior, you may also need to follow up with a restraining order. I hope you never have to be in this position. But if so, do whatever you need to do to keep yourself safe. Sometimes people do go over the edge and become nuts when they really recognize they've lost someone. Remember: not all chumps are abusive or crazy, but some are. So don't get paranoid, but do pay attention.

Again, these are just a few methods. Be creative, as long as you stick to the basic guidelines:

- ✦ Make "I" statements and avoid "you" statements.
- ✦ Keep the communication as simple and direct as possible.
- ✦ Use action words rather than feeling words.
- ✦ Keep your emotions to yourself. He's not worthy of being privy to your feelings anymore.

✦ Don't give mixed messages allowing hope for the future. If you're still holding onto hope, keep this to yourself.

✦ Refrain from inviting him to express his side of things. You've already heard it many times.

✦ Act strong, even if you feel weak. Share your vulnerabilities with people whose actions show they truly care about you.

This is most likely going to be a very painful experience for you. But just like going to the gym after a long hiatus can create a lot of muscle soreness, the pain will get easier and easier over time. Before you embark on the actual method, get feedback from a trusted friend. But in the end, do what's best for you.

Quick Recipe Guide for Step One

✦ Examine all possible breakup methods and do a pros and cons list on each one.

✦ Review your pros and cons lists (preferably with a good friend) and select the method you will use.

✦ Once you've chosen your method, practice it. If you've decided to mail/e-mail a letter or talk on the phone, write out several versions and get a trusted friend's opinion. You may have to revise it several times. In fact, on the first round, write everything you'd like to tell him were he someone who would actually take your feelings into account and validate you without being defensive. This is the fantasy letter. Then, after you're done with that, revise, revise, revise, until you are down to just a few sentences. You can also do this exercise for a face-to-face chat. Practice in the mirror or talk to his photo. If you've chosen the Houdini method, you can still do this exercise, though you won't actually be delivering any message to him. Plus, you could visualize what you'll do if he contacts you and possibly catches you off guard.

✦ Enlist your support network. Let all your best friends and loved ones know that you're going to make the break and that you'll need their strength and support for the next couple of weeks, especially over the next several days. It's good to set up actual check-in times when you know they'll be available. You have nothing to be ashamed of for needing to rely on your friends to help pull you out of this. People who love you will be happy to nurture you when they can. Just be respectful that people have busy lives and may not be available 24/7. That's why you want to engage as many people as you can so that you don't burn out anyone or cause people to start avoiding you because you've become too much of a drain. Usually when people have been asked in advance about their availability, they'll be far more inclined to offer what they can.

✦ Implementation time. Once you feel ready, take action with your chosen method. Send the letter, make the call, or cancel your phone number and change your e-mail address. If you're meeting him face-to-face, set up the time with him as soon as he's available. Then pull the plug and do it! Once finished, call or e-mail all who are in your support network.

As an added precaution, for sure, quickly delete his number from speed-dial and your IM list. There's no reason to keep him so quickly accessible. Also, if feasible, put him on the blocked senders list of your e-mail. Unless you have a darn good reason to have to stay in contact (and I do mean a darn good reason, like you have kids), do whatever you can to keep your distance. You're going to have moments of doubt and fear of being without him, and you don't want to make it easier for yourself in these times to get back in touch with him!

✦ Keep yourself as busy as you can. Don't hide in the bed. Best to be with loved ones, but if no one's available, get your butt out of the house and do errands, go to the movies, or finish a project you've set aside for a rainy day. Do not contact him. I repeat: do not contact him. Every cell of your body will want to reach out to him. You've been programmed to think of his needs and feelings as more important than your own. But it's time to make yourself important. Going to him for comfort would be like shooting yourself in the foot. He can't make this pain go away. Only you can.

While I strongly discourage you from indulging in any self-destructive behaviors, if you must rely on certain less-than-ideal crutches or habits to get you through this step (for a day or two), then okay. Anything is better than trying to reach out to him. Of course, any lethal drugs or seriously risky behaviors are off-limits. But an extra glass of wine or two (assuming you're not driving) or several pieces of your favorite chocolate/candy probably won't do any long-term damage if you don't have any preexisting health conditions.

The temptation to throw in the towel and lose all concern for taking care of yourself may be particularly high just after you make the break. It's understandable to have these feelings given the type of relationship you've endured. But you simply must resist acting on any impulses to harm yourself. You may not believe life is worth living without him at this moment, but you'll soon see that not only is it worth living, it's actually a heck of a lot better without him.

Chapter 6

{ step two }

Transforming Self-Downers to Self-Uppers

Starting from here forward, we're going to make a change in the language we use to identify the chump. No longer will we be referring to the guy you've just dumped as *your* chump. From here on in, he's *the* or *that* chump, or any other name you choose to give him. What he's not is anything you continue to have any stake in. So refrain from using words implying any kind of possession or belonging to each other. This may seem trivial. But actually the words we use can have a lot of power over how we feel about things.

It's normal and natural to use possessives (mine, ours, yours) when referring to your mate. But it becomes counterproductive to your mission of healing to say anything that implies attachment when dealing with a chump. Thus, it's a good idea to use words of detachment when you're no longer officially together. Referring to him as *that* or *the* chump enhances the experience of disconnecting. It paves the way to recognizing that you're now formally single! Of course, this may take some practice and getting used to. But you must become as conscious as you can of your tendency to keep the relationship alive in your mind. And watching your language is a good first step.

Granted, I'm well aware that you may not have actually applied the last chapter's advice and, thus, haven't yet made the final break. You might still be mulling over the idea, wanting to read through this entire book first before taking any action. That's okay! You've gotta do what works best for you. I trust at some point you'll be ready to take action, and then all of these tips and tools will be right at your fingertips and fresh in your mind. So I'll just keep on going, and you catch up at your own pace.

In order to get to the next step to stop pining, fantasizing, and romanticizing you must first identify the bullshit you've been selling yourself and transform these distortions into actual reality; you need to get rid of self-downers and exchange them for self-uppers. Then you will actively identify what didn't work in the relationship and find tools to reprogram your brain to get his picture off your favorites list.

Self-Downers: Irrational, Negative Distortions

Here's the deal. Whether you've been aware of this or not, you've been feeding your emotional brain a whole bunch of lies. Don't worry. I'm not calling you a liar in the classically negative sense. I don't think you've done anything consciously malicious. But you have held on to faulty beliefs about yourself and the chump. And unless you 'fess up to these distortions, you're going to remain stuck pining for him and romanticizing the relationship.

It's par for the course to have inflicted emotional damage on yourself while involved with a chump, most likely because you didn't think you were "all that" even before you ever met the guy. You haven't been able actually to live the words "I deserve better." Probably, you've had trouble even believing this statement to be true. But just remember: you absolutely can reverse the damage once you start naming the truth.

Think of this scenario. Imagine for a moment that you've become blind—gosh forbid, but just go with me here. You learn how to navigate your neighborhood with a special cane, and you work hard at developing your other senses so that you're comfortable in your immediate surroundings. You're doing fine, and then one day the only grocery store where you shop for all your nutritional and personal needs changes owners and becomes a small convenience store. No more fresh vegetables or fruits, no array of meats, fish, and dairy—just a few essentials. You don't ask whether there's another store nearby because you're too afraid to venture outside of your familiar territory. So instead you convince yourself that frozen peas are your favorite vegetable. And, "Who needs a variety of breads? Carbs suck anyway!" you tell yourself. So you downsize all of your preferences and make your reality fit into what you've become accustomed to.

In many ways, staying with a chump is very similar to being blind and only having one small store to meet all your needs. Fear and a negative self-image keep you stuck in a small space even when a whole new and far more enriched territory is right at your fingertips. In other words, the chump is not your only source of nourishment. In fact, he's a very poor one at that! And just like a blind person can learn to trust her other senses to expand her horizons, you too can learn to move beyond familiar territory.

Selma, a twenty-three-year-old production assistant, had a stormy affair with Kent, a much older gentleman, while on location shooting a movie. He was the be-all and end-all to her loneliness and overall dissatisfaction with her life. Of course, he forgot to mention that he was married at the time they started their intense flirtation. Though she loved their connection, she'd been raised never to step on another woman's territory—believing that doing so would seriously screw with her karma. So with great disappointment, she ended their affair.

Shortly after she returned home from the set, she decided she was done with the movie industry and wanted to get onto a more "serious" career path. She decided to go back to school and finish her degree in communications. Of course, being quite an attractive woman, she had no problem drawing the attention of male suitors. What she lacked, however, was a good "picker." Hence she ended up accepting offers from a lot of jerks. She'd date a guy for a couple of weeks or so and then move on to another, becoming increasingly lonely and pessimistic about her love life potential.

Then she met Doug, a twenty-five-year-old prelaw student. Doug caught Selma's attention in the cafeteria while they were both making a mad dash for the lunch special—turkey sandwich and homemade soup. He was tall, muscular, and definitely hot! And he had the greatest smile she'd ever seen.

They talked for hours, both brushing off their classes for the afternoon. They started dating very quickly and promised exclusivity within the first few weeks of having met each other. Doug appeared strong and confident, and all Selma could think about was having his big, strong arms wrapped around her.

Things were great between them for several months. But then something started to change—not drastically at first but enough to raise an eyebrow or two. Whereas Doug had initially seemed so positive and even-tempered, especially around his friends, he became increasingly moody and ill-tempered, particularly when they were alone together. Selma kept chalking up his moods to stress because of his intense coursework and upcoming applications for law school. At first, he would snap at her, blaming her for his foul attitude, but he'd quickly apologize when she'd stand up for herself. But as time progressed, his snappiness escalated, and his apologies virtually disappeared.

Because Doug had presented so well, or so she thought, she was shocked by his transformation. And she kept thinking *she* must be doing something wrong. But in hindsight, he had displayed grizzly-type behavior from the beginning. For one, he had disclosed to her that he'd been kicked out of another college for poor performance and drug use, and that he was currently on probation at the college they both attended. He'd also had his driver's license suspended on a few occasions, and he'd been in several bar fights since he'd turned twenty-one. Sometimes, when they'd been out late at night, he'd shown signs of being out of control, but Selma justified his actions as just being those of a guy who needed to let off some steam.

Doug also had talked very negatively about his previous girlfriend, referring to her with all kinds of lovely labels such as "total controlling bitch." Of course, once Selma had the opportunity to meet his ex, she discovered that the gal was very pleasant and rather sweet. She had just been so fed up with all the insanity in her relationship with Doug that she appeared to be a nag when, in fact, all she was ever doing was asking Doug to live up to his end of the relationship.

Unfortunately, rather than leaving the relationship, once Selma became privy to his real personality, she convinced herself that she could tame him by simply loving him more. Sound familiar? But this strategy backfired. And wouldn't you know it? He started calling her a "controlling bitch."

Selma stayed with Doug and tolerated his aggressive and hostile behavior for almost two years. Essentially, she continued to try to get her groceries from a poorly stocked store, and just like the example of the blind woman, she was too frightened to venture out and find another source for food. But just as you will soon enough, Selma finally saw the light. And as if struck by lightning, she woke up one morning knowing that if she wanted to have a happy romantic life, she'd better get out of the relationship with Doug. She understood she needed to fill up her own holes, get out of denial, and stop justifying his behavior by telling herself lies.

It never ceases to amaze me how clever women can be about how to spin a situation so that they are at fault, even when they have no responsibility in it whatsoever. Though the list of distortions is endless, some of the more popular ones we women sell ourselves when we've been with a chump include:

- ✦ He's the only guy for me.
- ✦ No one will ever love me like he does.
- ✦ I will never again have the kind of chemistry I have with him.
- ✦ If he doesn't want me, no one ever will.
- ✦ I must be a failure or this relationship would have worked.
- ✦ I don't deserve to be loved.
- ✦ I have too many needs.
- ✦ I've ruined his life. He won't survive without me.
- ✦ I'm an inadequate lover.

Do any of these sound familiar? Do you have others that swirl around in your head? Take a moment and really think about all the lies you've sold yourself. But be careful not to shame yourself. Shame only keeps the blinders on. If you really want to face the music of what you've been doing to yourself so that you can finally stop, you must examine your beliefs in a loving, open, and curious way.

So let's get to work on shifting these distortions as quickly as possible. First, make your own comprehensive list of all the negative beliefs you've sold yourself during the course of the relationship with the chump. Try to include both the distortions about yourself and about him. You're certainly welcome to use the list I've provided above if these fit, but please take the time to make it as personally relevant to you as possible. Delete what doesn't fit and add to it.

Next, read the following statement aloud.

I deserve to feel good about myself and to have people in my life who actually treat me well. I deserve respect and kindness from a partner, and I will offer the same. At no point from here forward will I accept another mate who doesn't act lovingly, no matter how much he professes his love. I am making a commitment to myself to take care of my part in building my self-esteem so that I will become a magnet for a positive, nurturing mate.

Now it's time to take each distortion and turn it into a reality statement. I will use the list I've provided above as an example.

He's the only guy for me.

Part of what makes us successful at having monogamous intimate relationships is the ability to distort reality a little bit in order to keep our attention focused on the mate we've chosen to be with. If we walked around thinking that there's always someone better around the corner, we wouldn't be able to permanently hook up with anyone. We'd be living in that wondering state often known as "the grass is always greener" syndrome. But the operative words here are "distort reality a *little* bit."

Once you discover you've given your heart to a chump, then this distortion is no longer adaptive, and even quite harmful. In your situation the grass truly is greener on the other side. In fact, it's not only greener, it's plusher, softer, and more durable. And it looks good even when it hasn't been mowed for a couple of weeks!

Betsi and Nick moved in together after a year of dating. He'd lived with a couple of other guys in a small apartment, and she was tired of being around a bunch of sloppy bachelors whenever she went over to his place. He ended up spending most of the nights at her place anyway so it seemed to make sense to cut their expenses by sharing a space. With Nick moving into her place and paying half her rent, she'd be saving money, and she believed she'd be happier. What Betsi had failed to consider was that the behaviors associated with Nick's living with a bunch of guys weren't going to change just because he changed locations. But Betsi had convinced herself that the other guys were a negative influence, that Nick would break his bad habits once away from them. I bet you can guess how this story goes. But I'll tell you anyway.

Nick was basically a pig-type chump who also leaned heavily on the sloth side as well. What she had observed while he was living with his buddies emerged in full force in their shared space. Nick never picked up after himself. He would sometimes spend an entire weekend on the couch without doing anything but watching TV, going to the bathroom, and ordering in take-out food. If Betsi complained and asked him to go out and do something with her, he'd reply, "Sure, honey, after this program is over." But, lo and behold, there'd be another program, then another.

Nick often missed work to go play golf with the guys, and he was looked over for many promotions because he simply wasn't demonstrating noteworthy performance. When they'd first gotten together, Nick had shared many dreams. But it turned out to be all talk and no action.

Betsi tried everything. At first she took the soothing, concerned approach, wondering whether Nick might be suffering from some kind of depression. And she offered to seek help with him. He shrugged this off, giving it no merit. And besides, he did seem to find time to play with his friends and muster up enough energy to go to Las Vegas or elsewhere out of town when one of his friends was getting married. He just didn't seem to have any interest in spending time with Betsi.

Next Betsi tried the hard-line ultimatum approach. She told Nick that she had no interest in being his maid or his mother, and if he didn't start cleaning up his own messes and spending some time with her, she wasn't going to have sex with him anymore. Not that this approach would have worked anyway since this guy clearly had no respect for her or her needs, but Betsi wasn't able to follow through with her threats anyway. She feared he'd hook up with someone else on the side, and the threat of that was far too frightening.

Last, she tried pleading. She told him how much she suffered and how much she loved him. "Wouldn't you please try to pay attention to me for a change," she would beg, letting him know she'd do whatever he wanted in return. What she had trouble realizing was that this guy was too darn selfish and immature to care about her needs.

As you can imagine, Betsi's self-worth continued to plummet. She'd become so skilled at blaming herself for Nick's behavior that she completely lost sight of the fact that the grass *would* be greener somewhere else (no doubt about it!). Thankfully, after some of her closest friends stepped in and read her the riot act, she came to her senses.

Betsi finally ended the relationship and told Nick he had to move out. Guess what he said to her? He had the nerve to ask her to front him a couple thousand dollars so he could go get a nicer place of his own. She was tempted to bite the bait at first, believing that he would be so appreciative of her generosity he would change his ways. But fortunately she began to see the insanity of this logic. She held her ground and kicked him out!

Not surprisingly, Nick moved back in with his buddies. Betsi ran into one of his friends a couple of years later. And guess what? He was still living in a pigsty, regularly replacing remote control batteries. Betsi, on the other hand, had become engaged to an up-and-coming financial analyst who actually put his shoes in the closet and his dirty socks in the hamper!

As you can see there are many guys other than a chump. You just have to be willing to hold out for one and distinguish the good ones from the bad ones.

No one will ever love me like he does.

The best retort I have to this distortion is "Thank goodness no one will ever love you like he does because his love is worthless to you." I don't mean to sound harsh, but this is true. Love from a chump is worse than no love at all. In fact, the longer you persist in calling whatever the chump sold you "love," the longer you will be confused about what true love is.

Rachel had been emotionally abused by her father. No matter what she would do to win his approval and positive regard, he would always find fault with her. He constantly rubbed in her mistakes, demanding perfection. When she would bring home a stellar report card, he'd find the one area of imperfection and comment on that. She would often cry in her room, feeling unloved.

Her dad would hear her sobbing and he would tell her that she shouldn't be weak. He was only telling her these things because he "loved" her and he wanted her to grow up to be a successful, responsible adult. He had no concept that he was basically setting the stage for her to confuse love with abuse. Even her mother would convince her that her dad was only being hard on her for her own good and that she should appreciate how much he did for her.

Rachel, like most of us, was taught early on to respect her parents and to look to them for information about the world. After all, parents are our most important teachers in life. In a healthy, loving home, we're invited to ask questions and explore our own solutions. But in an abusive or dysfunctional home, we're never to question the wisdom of authority no matter how bizarre it may seem. So over the years, Rachel grew to believe that being loved doesn't have to feel good. If someone says he loves you, then it must be true, no matter how unloving the love feels.

Rachel wasn't allowed to date while she was in high school. And even though she could date once she was eighteen, she didn't really want to. For one, she felt inadequate, not having had any experience. And since she remained at home, working part-time and attending a local junior college, she was too busy anyway. Plus, she didn't think her dad would make it very easy for her should she actually like someone. So she put off exploring Cupid's arena until she went off to a university.

Rachel dated a few guys during her college years, but nothing serious. For a while she was too afraid to let anyone get too close to her. Until she met Brandon, a twenty-year-old snake-type.

Brandon was smoother than smooth. He seemed to know everything she was feeling and thinking before she'd even say anything. He understood that she had some self-esteem problems, and he promised her that if she stuck with him, she'd be feeling good about herself in no time. He would be her savior.

For the first several weeks Rachel and Brandon were inseparable. He took her to all his favorite places, constantly praising her and buying her little gifts. Rachel could not have had any idea this guy was a snake. He was simply too good to be true.

Yep, that's exactly what he was—too good to be true. It was all an act. He was one of those really creepy predator types, seeking out women who feel bad about themselves. He'd dive in and boost their self-image and then go in for the kill the minute the woman would start showing signs of having a self. After about a month, Rachel shared an opinion of her own, contrary to Brandon's, and then criticism and insults quickly replaced the praise. At first his comments were more subtle, but as time went on his attacks became more and more stinging, putting her in an even lower place of self-worth than before they'd met.

Brandon would pick on her for the littlest things and tease her relentlessly if she spoke up about something she didn't know too much about. He was the expert in everything, and she was supposed to rely on him for confidence and guidance. The unspoken but very clear message was that she was not to have a mind of her own.

Of course as any good snake knows, you can't give away all your venom at once. You have to give it in appropriate doses. And Brandon was a master at his game. So every once in a while, he'd supply her with a boost of affection and attention. And just like Rachel's father had said, Brandon would tell her that he was only hard on her because he wanted her to be the best person she could be. "If I didn't really love you, I would have dumped your ass by now," he would reply to her attempts to seek reassurance. Can you believe it? But because Rachel had been programmed to believe that love comes in a painful package, she stuck around for more than a year.

It took a couple of months of therapy for Rachel to realize that she had been emotionally abused by her father, and that she was now allowing the same thing to happen to her by staying with Brandon. Fortunately, she quickly realized that while she didn't have the power to change what she'd endured as a kid and she certainly didn't have many choices while growing up, as an adult it was up to her to create the love life she desired. And staying with Brandon wasn't going to cut it. Plus, she had the power to leave *him*.

So the distortion *No one will ever love me like he does* needs to be dumped along with the chump. There are plenty of guys who will treat you badly, but there are also many who will treat you with the care you deserve. And again, it's actually a really good idea not to search out the kind of love a chump provides.

I will never again have the kind of chemistry I have with him.

Unfortunately, I really can't argue you out of this one. But I will say that you may want to seriously rethink whether you want this kind of chemistry again. It's highly possible that the chemistry you felt with the chump has a lot more to do with familiar angst you endured in childhood and distortions about what good chemistry is. And there is definitely a difference between good and bad chemistry. Good chemistry leads to enduring passion and positive excitement. Bad chemistry, albeit very intense, leads to anxiety, chronic uneasiness, insecurity, and fear about what the future will hold. Good chemistry enhances life; bad chemistry leads to toxic destruction.

Dorian, a thirty-two-year-old actress, proved to be a bit of an adrenaline junky. She loved fancy cars, staying out late, and trying anything new just for the kick of it. Not surprisingly, she'd fall for guys who liked to make a big splash in her life—whisking her away to exotic places. But she discovered that this fast-paced life, heavily focused on material things, wasn't bringing her happiness. And she eventually realized that the chemistry she sought with these flashy guys inevitably turned into painful nights of crying and despair.

Rick, a highly successful musician, was the last straw. Sure, no one would disagree that Dorian and Rick were a sizzling couple. But the sizzle often heated up to scorching flames, searing her heart and her trust in men. Rick was about as chumpy as they come. On any given day, he could fit the category of any of the prototypes: snake, grizzly bear, weasel, pig, or sloth. Some days he was as nice as can be, other days a tyrant. Some days he wanted to play, and play hard, but then he would isolate and retreat completely. It's highly possible he suffered from bipolar disorder (a serious mental condition characterized by periods of extreme depression alternating with periods of extreme mania). But it really didn't matter, because he wouldn't seek help no matter how much Dorian pleaded with him to do so.

Though some people seem to have a higher need for stimulation and excitement than others, probably due to temperament, in Dorian's case a lot of her adrenaline-seeking behavior grew out of having lived in a highly chaotic family. There was constant fighting and yelling between her parents and from her parents toward her. She wasn't able to remember any peaceful time growing up, except for the occasional visit she'd have with her maternal grandparents, who apparently had also been rather volatile. But at least in Dorian's presence and with their age, they were much more subdued.

It's no wonder that Dorian developed an inner model of relationships as tumultuous and unpredictable. She was so used to this emotional climate, she actually sought it out. And guys who were less "exciting," she deemed boring. But after her two and a half years with Rick, she'd come to her wit's end.

When Dorian came to see me she was in bad shape emotionally. Her body had been showing signs of tremendous stress. She had been losing clumps of hair, feeling nauseous much of the time, and unable to concentrate. She was even having trouble remembering her lines, something that generally came quite easy to her. She wasn't sleeping well, and she experienced chronic anxiety all day long. She was basically in a state similar to what she'd experienced for the bulk of her childhood.

Once Dorian was able to understand that what she called chemistry was actually toxicity, she recognized that she needed to search for a different emotional experience than the one she had with Rick. She still loves living in the fast lane, but she's learned that excitement and elation need to be balanced with groundedness and security—otherwise she's cooking up a recipe for disaster.

If he doesn't want me, no one ever will.

There's no way you'd ever be able to convince me that no one else in the whole wide world would ever find you desirable. No matter how pathetic, homely, or damaged you believe you are, this just simply can't be true. Maybe you do in fact need to improve your self-image in order to attract a worthy mate, but it absolutely isn't the case that no one will ever want you again.

If you're prone to this distortion, you need to be especially careful you don't turn it into a self-fulfilling prophecy. In other words, if you believe you're unlovable, you will direct your actions accordingly, oftentimes causing the very thing you fear the most. Your irrational belief may become a reality, not because it was ever true but because you've pushed interested parties away and then used this as evidence that you're someone who gets chronically rejected. The reality however is that you've been doing the rejecting, perpetuating your belief that no one will ever want you. A vicious cycle ensues!

I've seen this happen a number of times with women who hold on to this distortion after a breakup, convincing themselves that they're truly unlovable. What they often don't see is that they're creating what they fear. They stop flirting, hide out on weekends and after work, and never smile at strangers. They stop going to places where they might meet someone. Or they camouflage their belief in their own undesirability by finding fault in anyone who actually does express interest.

After Leslie dumped John and felt ready to go back out on the dating scene she struck out over and over again. She hadn't truly shifted her belief that no one but John would ever want her. Rather she'd simply covered up her insecurity and decided she'd give it another go. And, boy, did she. She signed up for every on-line dating service and joined every organization geared toward singles. She'd have made a great spokesperson for any organization aimed at dating. She was out there to the fullest. However because of this buried belief, she never made it past a first date with anyone. That's when she came to my office. She said, "I did what everyone told me to do. I put myself back out there and started dating. I did exactly what they said, and I was totally right.

No guy will ever want me. I should never have broken up with John. At least he loved me."

What Leslie failed to volunteer was the fact that it was actually she who was finding fault with every guy who expressed interest in her. It wasn't at all true that no guy found her interesting. She came from the belief that any good guy who would want her must actually be a complete loser or geek. So why even bother?

The lesson to learn from Leslie is that you must actively deal with the distortion and really make it go away. Don't let your fears get the best of you. Nip them in the bud by seeing the insanity in the distortion.

I must be a failure or this relationship would have worked.

Okay, do you really want to sell yourself this crock of shit? Or might there be an alternative? Let's allow the facts in the relationship to provide the verdict. How many times did you try to make things better? How many times did you change your own needs, opinions, and feelings just to accommodate him? For how long did you put up with promises of change? Now based on your responses, who really did the failing?

As I've stated and implied many times—but it's certainly worth doing again—you cannot be responsible for anybody else's behavior but your own. You cannot control other people unless they allow you to. (Granted, if you put someone in a victim position by holding a gun to his head, you certainly could get him to do what you want, but that's only under extreme conditions of powerlessness.) He did not make you stay with him. And you did not make him be the asshole that he is. He did that all on his own. So don't in any way take this burden on your shoulders. Sure you may have had a role in why the relationship didn't work out, but my hunch is that you repeatedly attempted to fix your part of what wasn't working well, and he continued to be a chump.

Taking responsibility for your part is something to continue to preserve for your next relationship, but that will be with someone who's worthy of your efforts and not with a chump who will simply exploit your changes. So at any moment that this faulty belief invades your thoughts, say "STOP" in your head and remind yourself of how little the chump did for you. If anything, he should be feeling like he's the failure. But don't hold your breath. The most important thing is that you don't give this distortion any more power.

I don't deserve to be loved.

I don't want to be too presumptuous, but I'm almost certain that if you believe you don't deserve to be loved, you have a long history of very low self-esteem that far predates the relationship with the chump. You probably believe the only reason you were even able to have a relationship with anyone was because either you were able to fool him into thinking you were worthy and/or you were lucky.

Let me ask you this. Is there anyone in your life whom you care about that you believe doesn't deserve to be loved? I doubt it. And you know what? I bet that no one else who cares about you believes that about you either. This is only in your own head, and I would venture a guess that someone important to you in your childhood treated you in a way that either stripped away your self-worth or interfered with the development of any self-esteem at all.

Please make a commitment right now to toss this ever-so-destructive way of thinking out of your life. You absolutely do deserve love. But in order to find someone who's worthy of loving you, you must endorse yourself. Say the words "I deserve to be loved" every hour of the day. Write the sentence on Post-its and stick them all over your living space. Go out and get some self-affirmation books or tapes and start using them right away!

I have too many needs.

It's definitely possible that you are too needy in a relationship if you're expecting someone else to meet and fulfill all your needs. But that can easily be remedied by taking responsibility for getting your needs met by you. (Okay—maybe not so easily, but certainly doable.) But it's not true that you have too many needs. It's all relative.

Of course you're going to feel like you have too many needs when you're with a chump, even if you are really good at fulfilling them yourself. A chump doesn't want you to need anything from him, and he's highly likely to tell you you're too needy even when you're just expecting the bare minimum. Or he wants you to be completely dependent on him but then doles out his "love" according to his decisions.

On the flip side, if you're with a guy who respects your needs and doesn't shame you for them, and he's good at giving where he can, then you're not going to experience your needs as a big deal. They just are what they are.

Alison fell in love with Bruce. They both shared a love of adventure, great food, and laughter. Then she discovered he was a weasel-type. On the surface he was fun and games, and when he was physically present he was a really good time. But he could not be pinned down, and he frequently missed their dates. While he loved a good conversation if he initiated it, he selfishly denied Alison any attention when she wanted contact with him. The relationship ran on his terms and his needs. No wonder Alison felt too needy. Fortunately Alison didn't stay too long in that relationship, having already learned a lesson or two from past relationships with good-time guys. And once she got involved with Jeremy, she finally had the experience she deserved.

Jeremy loved Alison's desire to be with him. He felt honored to be in her company and thought she was a true gift in his life. At first Alison had no idea what to do with this kind of positive treatment, and of course she kept waiting for the axe to fall. But Jeremy proved to be a consistently loving guy who reciprocated Alison's needs for contact. Wow! What a treat for Alison. She no longer felt she had to hide her desire to be in the company of her guy. See what I mean? In one context you might seem too needy, whereas in another, your needs are simply embraced.

Alison, however, still had a hole in the bottom of her cup, and the cup remained empty, no matter what Jeremy did to fill it. Alison needed to seal the bottom so that she would experience the good things coming in her direction. And for some of her needs—those she felt ashamed of—she had a particularly hard time finding comfort from any source But once she grew more secure in her loving relationship with Jeremy, she was able to cork the bottom and actually hold onto the good stuff.

I've ruined his life. He won't survive without me.

You do not have the power to ruin a guy's life unless you hold him hostage and make him dependent on you for his survival needs. And I highly doubt that you participated in any such prisoner-of-war games. Just as he can't be the sole source of your happiness and he doesn't have the power to ruin your life, you shouldn't hold yourself responsible for what happens to him. The guy had and has choices for what to do with his life, just as you have choices about yours. I don't mean to sound insensitive, but if he doesn't survive without you, which I highly doubt, then that's because he chooses not to. Besides, most chumps simply move on to other willing prey. Unfortunately as long as women continue to be plagued by low self-esteem and society continues to condone toxic male behavior, then there's always going to be another willing participant for him to pounce on.

Granted, some behaviors qualify as far more toxic than others. And the chump you've dumped may be of the milder ilk. But you still have nothing to feel guilty about unless you've actually done something wrong, like threatening him with harm. Even if you've resorted to such desperate measures, unless you've actually followed through with the threats, you still don't have to hold yourself responsible for his actions henceforth. Regardless, it's not going to help you move forward with your life if you dwell on how he's going to manage his. Do you think he's sitting around wondering whether he's ruined your life? And even the most remote chance that he is, then why didn't he try to make things better when you were actually a couple? These are the types of questions to ask yourself to give you a hefty dose of reality: You did not ruin his life!

I'm an inadequate lover.

This is a classic distortion, especially if the chump you dumped cheated on you. One of the first places we go in our minds when a lover is unfaithful is "What's wrong with me?"

Even if the guy didn't cheat, we women frequently interpret a situation as our fault due to some inherent deficiency.

Maybe the guy actually told you he thought you were inadequate in the sack. But remember the source. He's a chump. Would you go to a crazy person to check your car engine if it started making funny noises? I highly doubt it. So don't expect to get an accurate diagnosis of what's wrong in a relationship from a chump. You're only going to get put-downs, criticism, and hostilities aimed at removing the focus of responsibility from the chump.

Frankly, I have no idea what kind of lover you are. But I seriously doubt you're inadequate. However, if you've had other people tell you so, or you believe you could brush up on your technique, that's not the end of the world. There are tons of classes, literature, courses, and books on sexuality and the art of lovemaking. Go check them out! Whatever you do, don't use anything he's told you as the final word. And if you're really honest with yourself, you'd probably admit that he was the one inadequate in bed since chumps notoriously aim to please only themselves. If you expressed any needs of your own, he would have likely seen you as selfish.

Also, many chumps are drawn to pornography. They'll tell you that all guys love porn and you should chill out about it. That's a topic for a whole other book. But suffice it to say that any guy who uses porn as the marker for a good lover has got serious issues, and you must not ever try to compete with porn images. You need a guy who appreciates you in the flesh, who desires to ravish your body with love and affection.

Creating Self-Uppers: Positive Actual Realities

Once you've identified your negative distortions, you must create a list of positive beliefs that are in line with actual reality, personalized to you. Use the nine most common distortions addressed above as a guide. Below are some examples.

He's the only guy for me. This statement can easily be transformed to: "He was not at all the guy for me. He's a chump, and I don't need or want a guy who treats me badly. I will no longer tolerate such bad treatment. The only guy for me will be one who respects me, loves me (the way I wish to be loved), likes my company, etc." (You fill in what you desire.)

No one will ever love me like he does. Change this to either "No one will ever love me like he did, thank goodness, 'cuz I don't want to be loved this way anymore" or "He didn't love me the way I want to be loved, and I don't need his kind of love."

I will never again have the kind of chemistry I have with him. I've already made the point on this in the discussion above. But just to remind you, on this one you say, "That's a relief, because this kind of chemistry will only kill me!"

If he doesn't want me, no one ever will. With this distortion, you simply respond with "That's bullshit!"

I must be a failure or this relationship would have worked. For this evil troublemaker you say, "I am a great success because I'm finally free. Way to go, me!"

I don't deserve to be loved. For this bad boy, respond with "Take a hike. I'm tired of you putting me down. I deserve to be loved like everyone else. Most important, I deserve to be loved by me!"

I have too many needs. This one's a bit tricky because if you've endured a life of too much hardship or mistreatment then you've been in a state of deprivation for far too long, and it could very well appear that you have too many needs. You must reframe this statement to acknowledge that you have unmet needs, but that this is not equivalent to having too many. Once you accept that it is your job to fulfill your needs and to steer clear of people who shame you for them, then you won't be too much of a handful. So the key is to not go to empty wells for water if you're thirsty. If you stay too long in a dry desert, you're going to become quickly dehydrated and parched. Then when you finally find a water source, you'll likely push anything or anyone out of your way to have a drink. You'll in fact appear to be a greedy, bottomless pit. So don't put yourself in this position in the first place. Instead, always have ample resources to satiate your needs.

Once you see that there's nothing available for you, then it's your job to get yourself to a place that offers the supplies you need. Keep your expectations of other people reasonable. I'll talk more about this later when you're ready to seriously consider the type of mate you desire. For now change this statement to: "I'm responsible for my needs and for creating relationships with people who facilitate my ability to meet them and who offer support and nurturance."

I've ruined his life. He won't survive without me. On this one, you simply must get over your sense of grandiosity. I know you're coming from a place of concern and empathy, but you're simply not that powerful. And the more you accept this notion of your limitations, the better chance you have of letting go of any unconscious or conscious beliefs that other people are responsible for ruining your life. You have to trust me on this one. I had lived a good part of my life feeling responsible for everyone else's feelings. And the unconscious contract I'd made (which no one had ever signed, by the way) was that other people were responsible for my happiness because I was taking on the burden of theirs. This way of thinking creates a victim spiral, where you remain dependent on other people and you're bound to be continually disappointed.

So stop the cycle right now by claiming the following statement instead: "I'm responsible for my own life and other people are responsible for theirs. I'm not powerful enough to be able to ruin someone's life nor is someone else powerful enough to ruin mine." Of course, if you're in charge of a true dependent, like a child or a sick elderly person, this statement doesn't apply. But as long as someone is of sound mind and has free will, he/she is responsible for his/her own choices. I'd bet on it that the chump you dumped met these two criteria.

I'm an inadequate lover. Let it go, girl! I can't imagine this to be true. But, hey, I've worked with lots and lots of women who've been molested, raped, violated, etc., and yeah, they do have some sexual hang-ups. I don't know whether you've experienced any such traumas that have resulted in problems expressing or enjoying your sexuality. Or you may not have endured any particular trauma, but maybe you were raised in a sexually repressive environment or didn't get the necessary sex education.

Whatever the circumstances, you have the power to boost your sexual appeal. You're not a child anymore and now, as an adult, you can fix whatever is broken. Most important, you're not inadequate, regardless of any sexual dysfunction. You have developed blocks to protect you, but you can certainly overcome your hardships. And besides, this is the last thing you should be worried about right now. You've got ample time to work on any of these old bruises once you've emotionally disconnected from the chump. So for right now, if this is one of your distortions, change it to: "I promise to embrace my sexuality to the fullest and be in charge of how I express it."

Beating the Temptation to Contact the Chump

Most likely, every cell in your body will command you to call or contact the chump. You'll be wondering what he's doing without you, whether he's as miserable as you are, and whether he's thinking about you and desperately missing you. You might even be tempted to go hunt him down, trying to spy on him at his usual hangouts or track his routines. The only thing I can tell you is DON'T.

For one, if you go after him after you've dumped him you lose all credibility. Even if he's pining for you, he'll see you as weak and be able to walk all over you once again. For another, you could appear to be a stalker and might actually get into trouble. Giving in to any obsessive thoughts will only keep you stuck.

Quick Recipe Guide
for Step Two

Get out of the house (in addition to going to work) and do something active. Get your body in motion. Go on a long walk with a friend, run up and down hills, or take a spinning class. Just do anything that triggers an endorphin release. No excuses, even if you have to sacrifice something else to make time for exercise. Because if you let a depression set in, you're going to be more vulnerable to losing your ground and making a hole for the chump to get back in. If you have any kind of physical disabilities, definitely check with your doctor before embarking on an activity you don't normally do. If your range of motion is restricted, then do what you can. Below are several more tools for step two.

✦ Make a To-Do List (TDL) of activities you can do instead of contacting the chump. Try to include at least ten items. Then when you're faced with the inevitable urge, keep going down the list until the temptation passes. Repeat as often as necessary. Just like with an addiction, you have to get through the withdrawal, and eventually the urges begin to subside. A sample list might include the following:

- ✦ Call my best friends (name three or four).
- ✦ Take a five-minute walk (all the while reminding myself I've left the chump for good reasons).
- ✦ Write in my journal for five minutes the top three reasons why I'm not with him anymore.
- ✦ Meditate.
- ✦ Accomplish a much overdue chore.
- ✦ Make plans for the day or evening.
- ✦ Do a favor for a friend or family member.
- ✦ Listen to music.
- ✦ Role-play how the conversation would probably go if I were to contact the chump.
- ✦ Go through that unread pile of mail.

The TDL is a very handy and quite effective tool, but you must use it. Your TDL becomes your quick reference guide for when you feel vulnerable to your urges to reconnect with the chump.

If you have thoughts pushing you to reach out for him, accept the thought as simply a thought. Thoughts don't have any power unless you supply energy to them. For example, if you think about lighting his car on fire, the thought has no impact unless you actually go out and pour gasoline all over it and toss a burning match on it. So don't be alarmed by any thoughts. Just let them pass. There can be no good outcome to reaching out to him. If you get back together with him, you'll only feel worse in the long run. And think how bad you'll feel if you contact him and he rejects you. No matter how badly you're hurting right now, you will feel better, and far more quickly if you just get through the withdrawal phase. I promise it will get easier.

✦ **Make a list of all your negative beliefs.** Give yourself ample time to add to your list as they occur to you. Keep a journal with you at all times so you can jot down whatever you notice throughout the day that belongs on your list.

✦ **Go through each item on your list and transform it into a positive,** using actual reality as your guide. Flesh out each one as fully as you can. The more meaningful you make these, the more they'll stick.

✦ **Think back on any times in your life when you thought of yourself in positive terms.** Use these memories as reminders that you are capable of feeling good. If you can't recall any experiences of positive self-regard, then just keep following the tools throughout the book and you should begin to reap the benefits. Also, add to your library by purchasing books or CDs on boosting self-esteem.

✦ **Diligently practice accepting the positive statements you've created.** Run down your list every few hours and recite them aloud. Tell your friends to remind you of your value. Decorate a box and put positive affirmations inside. Whenever you're feeling down, reach inside the box and read one of the items.

✦ **Give yourself a huge pat on the back.** Even if you fell off the wagon and made contact with him, I'm certain you've at least resisted a time or two. Any efforts and progress deserve acknowledgment. Take time to reflect on the tools that helped you main-tain distance from the chump. Keep the ones that worked well for you handy so you can continue to rely on them as the urges continue.

Now, let's move on to the next chapter, where you will learn to stop pining for, fantasizing about, and romanticizing the chump.

Chapter 7

{ step three }

No More Pining for, Romanticizing, or Fantasizing About the Chump

I wouldn't be surprised if you've got chump-on-the-brain 24/7. After all, your energy has been consumed by this guy, functioning as his round-the-clock caregiver, accommodator, pacifier, and possibly even sex-slave. No doubt you were the one who did the work for both of you in the relationship. Successfully eliminating him from your thoughts will take some time.

I once had a friend tell me (concerning the relationship I was in at the time) that it was similar to watching a bad tennis match. Essentially, I'd booked the court, paid the fee, played both sides of the net, and then retrieved all the dead balls myself. Sure the chump rallied on occasion, but his contribution was so minimal, no one would have even noticed had he not shown up at all. Trust me, it wasn't a pretty sight!

Because you've been intensely invested in the chump, he's become like an addiction, or, at least, like a very bad habit. We all know how hard habits are to break! And breaking addictions can be even harder. So although you may wish to erase him from your memory, your brain may not cooperate initially. You haven't yet conditioned yourself to shut down all thoughts, feelings, or fantasies about him. Hence, your mind will pester you every minute of the day, even in your dreams, pushing you to get your fix. Until you train your brain otherwise, it will actively work against you, goading you on to think about him, contact him, and worst of all, make you believe you've made a big mistake by dumping him. You'll be continually seduced to believe you must get him back into your life.

Please don't despair! Think of a smoker trying to dump cigarettes. For a brief while, she will constantly think about having a cigarette. But the longer she can resist giving into the drive, the sooner the urges will start decreasing in both intensity and frequency. And because she knows that smoking increases her chances of getting cancer or, at the very least, shortening her life, she stays motivated to kick the habit. Likewise, because you're now fully aware that your chump damages your well-being, you know you must get rid of him, even though your heart hasn't yet fully grasped this reality.

Contrary to what you may believe, you can kick any bad habit or addiction. You simply must embrace the fact that you are in charge of your emotional mind by employing your rational mind. Then you can change your behavior, thereby delivering new information to your emotional brain, and resist the pressure to reunite with the chump. Essentially you must reprogram your thinking!

Understanding Needs

Before we move into the active exercises to help you quit pining for and fantasizing about the chump, it's important to first understand the differences between actual needs and preferences. While many people commonly mistake these as the same, they're not interchangeable. In fact, many of the things we describe as our *needs* are actually just preferences. And with preferences, we have many options, including the ability to live without. True, human beings have certain fundamental needs. Yet how we get them met, by whom, and in what quantities, varies greatly.

Clearly we all need food, water, and shelter for our basic survival. But while we must have nourishment and protection, we don't *have* to get these supplies from any one particular source. How we get our basic needs met comes through asserting preferences. For example, we can go to any supermarket, although I may prefer Ralphs whereas you prefer another food chain like Vons. Or you may choose to grow your own fruits and vegetables and catch your own fish to insure proper freshness, whereas another person may not mind prepackaged varieties. Oftentimes our own preferences change across time. For instance, regarding shelter, while I now prefer to live in a more rural area, at one point I totally thrived as a city girl and preferred to live in the midst of all the action.

We also have many emotional needs. We all need love, attention, approval, companionship, understanding, etc. But just like with our physical needs, these emotional needs can be met by a variety of people, and in many different ways. While we may prefer to get love from a specific person in a particular way, we can establish new relationships with others to insure these needs are met in ample supply. And the best news of all is that we almost always have the power to nourish ourselves and meet our own emotional needs. Hence while I may prefer my lover to rub my back when it aches, I don't actually need him for this. I could get a mechanical massager, or pay someone to knead my aches and pains.

Women who've been ensnarled in a relationship with a chump commonly argue that showering oneself with love doesn't feel the same as having an intimate partner give it. And I agree. Self-love is not the same as love from an intimate partner. But just because it's different doesn't mean it can't also have great value or feel just as good, especially once you see yourself as a worthy provider. Plus, being a reliable source to meet your own needs and preferences is a hell of a lot better than relying on a chump.

Understandably, right now your brain is trying to convince you that you need the chump. You've convinced yourself that you can't go on without him. But this simply isn't reality. You don't need *him* at all. The only thing you truly *need* at this moment is to stay as far away from him as possible so you can finally get on with your life and get ready for a good relationship. And soon enough, you'll also stop preferring him as well!

To help this concept stick, please start reciting the following statement several times a day:

I don't need the chump to supply any emotional longings. I may have preferred that he be the supplier, but he's been inadequate. I must take responsibility to search for better sources of love. I have a choice about where and how I get my needs fulfilled.

Of course, I encourage you to change up the words to fit your personality, but definitely make sure the message you send to your brain includes a distinction between needs and preference!

Retraining Your Brain

Have you ever been on a boat out at sea in rough waters? You'll notice that when you return to land it takes a while for your body to adapt to the new surface. You'll still feel like you're in motion, possibly for even longer than the time you spent at sea. Loving a chump is like sailing in stormy waters with no stabilizer or life preserver. It's a nasty experience, leaving you in a constant search for stable ground. But as awful as it can be, your body adapts to the motion, and it becomes the norm. Once you're finally out of the storm, you have to learn to walk on land again and get used to the stability. And this can be even harder if you've never been on stable ground because of a rough childhood and/or a series of tumultuous relationships. If that's the case, you'll be starting from scratch.

Anytime you take on a new challenge, like riding a bike or embarking on a regular exercise program, it takes awhile to condition yourself. So too does it take time to build and strengthen your emotional fitness. If you stick with it, though, the challenge gets easier and easier, and can eventually become part of your normal routine, just like brushing your teeth.

Until Laura understood that she had the power to turn off her pining meter, she sat around day in and day out thinking about Adam, the chump she'd dumped after their six-month fling. Adam, a guy in his late thirties, never married, presented himself as Mr. Wanna-Be Family Man. Laura, approaching thirty-two and eager to get married and have kids, believed Adam to be "the one."

During the first three months of their courtship, Adam behaved quite well. Laura was a little suspicious of him at first, wondering why such a great guy hadn't yet tied the knot with anyone. She dismissed the information she got right off the bat that not only had he never been married but he hadn't had any long-term relationships in more than ten years. He said he'd been focused on developing his career. He added that he didn't want to be in a relationship if he couldn't give it his all. But he assured her that he was ready for a deep commitment and she was the one he wanted to be with!

Laura was attracted to Adam's self-confidence and his ability to comfort her uncertainties. But somewhere around the four-month mark, Adam started pulling away. She asked him if something had changed, pointing out how distant he seemed. He convinced her it was all in her head, that he was just a bit preoccupied.

Eventually he told her that he was terrified of commitment, and he felt completely inadequate in the realm of relationships. His confessions of his insecurities were refreshing at first. And Laura believed that through her love and support she could easily help him overcome his fears. But Adam really wasn't interested in developing his relationship skills. Rather, he proceeded to become increasingly more withdrawn and isolated. Before she could figure out what was going on, he was acting as if Laura had somehow lassoed him into the relationship, with him having had no choice.

His behavior became more and more chumplike as the months continued. He reinvested all of his time and energy in his work and his hobbies. He made no efforts to see or spend time with Laura. And as is common to most chumps, he failed to take any responsibility for his actions.

Thankfully, through the coaxing from her friends Laura began to see that staying with Adam would be like signing up for a cruise across the Atlantic Ocean on a ship with a huge hole in its hull. After a couple of months of being last on his list of priorities, she knew it was time for her to cut her losses, lick her wounds, and jump ship. He'd essentially been passively breaking up anyway by often disappearing for days and failing to return her calls. She was just putting into formal action the writing on the wall.

What Laura didn't have were tools for how to get the bozo

off her mind. She became plagued with "what if" questions and thoughts. She'd go from "What if I'd been a little more patient?" to "What if I had not been so eager to hook up with him right away and had played the game of being disinterested?" to "What if I were to give him another chance?" Her "what ifs" were endless.

While the "what if" game caused her tremendous angst, she was equally plagued by "if onlys" (i.e., by totally mythical romantic fantasies of how wonderful their lives would be together if only she were to (*fill in the blank*). She became consumed with unreal pictures of something that would never happen for her if she were to stay with Adam.

In order to let go of Adam, Laura had to learn to stop airbrushing the relationship. She had to accept that the first three months of a relationship were hardly reflective of the ultimate quality of a long-term relationship with him. She had to come to terms with the fact that with a guy like Adam the honeymoon phase of their relationship bears no similarity to the long-term reality.

Laura learned that after a couple of months people generally feel more comfortable letting down their guard. That's when you are able to see who's really in front of you. Sometimes a great guy emerges, maybe a little different than the peacock, but one who would truly be a wonderful long-term partner. Not the case with Adam. (Nicely, Laura received poetic justice. Five years later, she found out Adam was still single.)

Just as Laura discovered, in order to stop pining for the chump, you must also stop fantasizing about him and quit romanticizing the relationship. You have to deal with reality. I know—easier said than done. Hey, I never said this would be an easy process, but it's certainly doable. And the sooner you stop romanticizing, the sooner you'll stop pining, and hence the sooner you'll be feeling better.

In order to come back to earth, you need to exchange the fantasies of what never actually transpired with present reality. You must put an end to the "what ifs" and "if onlys" and instead come up with "what else" or "what is."

Sometimes the "what if" deals specifically with him: What if I were to call him and apologize? Maybe he would give us another chance." Sometimes they're about making your own life seem catastrophic: "What if I never find another guy to love me again?" In either case the answer needs to be a "what else": "I could *not* call him and finally become free to move forward with my life, since I already know it's a dead-end road with him." Or, your answer to the fear of never being in love again would be: "Hey, I could find a guy who really loves me and treats me well."

"What ifs" are all speculative and usually concern an outcome we have no control over, like what the chump will do with his life now that you're not in it. So you might as well replace these negative projections with positive ones instead. Or, even better yet, stop projecting entirely and instead deal with what your goal is right now in front of you—getting over the chump and moving on.

Before you can do this, however, it helps to understand a bit about how the brain works. Here's a little experiment. In the next paragraph I have supplied you with an instructional exercise. Read the paragraph and then do what I suggest. Please do not read ahead until you've done what I've recommended. When you're finished you can read on. You need about five minutes to actually complete the exercise, so please no cheating! Don't worry, I won't ask you to do anything bizarre and may actually make you dumple a bit. Here we go.

Close your eyes and get into a relaxed position. For the next three or four minutes, I want you to think about anything but PEACHES. No matter what you do, do not think about how succulent they taste, how refreshing they are on a hot day, or the scent when you cut into one. Keep peaches out of your mind. NO peaches or peaches or peaches in your thoughts. Now go ahead and think quietly for a few minutes.

Okay, what's the first thing you thought about when you closed your eyes? Let me guess—peaches? That's okay, you couldn't help it. Anytime we tell ourselves we absolutely can't think about something, that's going to be the first thing we end up fixated on. Not to mention that if you have any issues with authority, you're bound to become rebellious to any orders, even if they're coming from yourself. Before you know it you'll be cutting off your own nose just to spite your face.

So how do you get yourself to stop thinking about the chump? The answer is you have to cut yourself some slack. If you want to stop pining for your chump you actually have to give yourself permission to take time to think about him. But you're now going to learn how to do this so that you actually get the desired result—fewer and fewer thoughts about him. The following exercises should help: "Selective Time," "The Stop Sign," "The Memory Box," "Redefining You," and "The Bead Jar."

Selective Time

First you need to schedule some time dedicated to thinking about the chump. You can pick any time you desire, but it can't be longer than thirty minutes, and you must decrease this time by increments of five minutes each time you practice this. I recommend you schedule uninterrupted time when you're able to give your full attention to your fantasies. Go ahead, indulge. After the time is up, spend a few more minutes writing down how you feel. Do you feel better or worse? How plausible are these fantasies knowing what you now know about the chump? Has he consistently demonstrated any of the qualities you ascribe to him in your romanticized picture? I somehow doubt it, or you wouldn't be in the position you're in.

When you do this exercise, avoid using the first few months you were together as the full representation of the relationship. The honeymoon period of a relationship (the time frame in which you perceive each other as relatively flawless) doesn't accurately reflect the quality of any relationship. For some couples this phase can last several months to several years, but inevitably the relationship enters a power-struggle phase. This usually happens very quickly with a chump, and the relationship fails because chumps either don't have the interest or the maturity necessary to work through this phase and move into true intimacy. So the first few months simply can't be used as the model. Even healthy couples never reclaim the initial bliss, because as I've said before, it's all based on projections.

Many years ago, I dated a guy for about six months. I'll call him Dick (how appropriate ☺). During the first month, we were on fire. He appeared kind, gentle, and humble. I was tired of the arrogant guys I'd typically dated and enjoyed the comfort of someone who would openly speak about insecurities and fears. He also saw me as the stronger one and told me he felt he could lean on me. Of course, his words at first were music to my ears, as I love to help vulnerable people. But I had no idea what I would be signing up for with Dick.

I had assumed that Dick would compliment my generous

spirit and that he would appreciate my gestures of kindness and willingness to comfort his fears. The reality was that he was setting me up to take care of him and never to expect anything in return. Naturally, during our honeymoon phase I couldn't see what was coming and he could do no wrong in my eyes. Of course I dismissed the many signals that should have alerted me right off the bat that this guy was going to be trouble—like the fact that he'd been engaged twice but never married, had serious financial problems due to very poor judgment, and frequently missed days at work so he could go off skiing, sailing, or surfing. It turned out that I was essentially the flavor of the month, and once he tired of me, he took his energy elsewhere.

Even though he was the one who had done a one-eighty, going from calling me ten times a day to not calling me for days, he pointed the finger at me, suggesting that I was too needy. I thought I'd signed up for a high-contact guy when, in fact, he was basically a loner who occasionally liked the adrenaline rush of pseudo-intimacy. I spent months fantasizing about what could have been between the two of us had he only remained the guy I fell head over heals for. I wasted so much time on something I had no control over.

To preserve my sanity, I had to face the music: he never was the guy I assumed he was. He loved to have fun and connect when he wanted to, but only on his terms. He had no insight into what would be good for the relationship, or for me. That was his flaw, not mine. And I needed to stop turning him into the saint and me into the damaged one. Absolutely, I'd become a needy, insecure cling-on, afraid he'd dump me at any moment. The reality was that he had used me and I had let him. No amount of wishing he were the guy I'd met was ever going to turn him around.

If you get fixated on something you did wrong in the relationship, own it. But don't use it against yourself. You must accept that the demise didn't happen in a vacuum. You've already assessed that he's a chump. Even if you had behaved perfectly, he probably still would have screwed up and been a bad partner.

The Stop Sign

Since you've only got a short, prescribed time to indulge in your fantasies, with less and less time progressively, you'll need something you can rely on continually to steer your brain clear of traveling down old, familiar unhealthy pathways. Every time you find yourself glorifying the chump or the relationship with him, imagine a big, red stop sign in your head and say these words:

Thanks for the memories, but no thanks! Trying to get me to romanticize a chump is counterproductive to my goal of changing my future. I want to have a loving relationship with someone who treats me as I deserve. I will no longer linger on old news.

Your mantra can be anything you want it to be as long as you emphasize that the thoughts of him are no longer welcome. Don't judge yourself or forbid yourself from having the thoughts. You don't have power over what pops into your head. But you do have control over whether or not you give the thoughts energy.

Once you've erected a stop sign in your mind and recited your mantra, it's time to steer yourself in another direction. You need to replace your delusional fantasy with one that actually can come true by imagining your ideal self and keeping him out of the picture altogether.

Of course, don't forget to use your To-Do List, or TDL! Go through all the items on your list and make sure to do them.

Your TDL works not only when you have the urge to contact the chump, but when you're pining for him as well.

The Memory Box

Except in very extreme cases, chumps usually aren't all bad. Many of them have some very nice qualities, and very possibly you two enjoyed some wonderful moments together. I don't want to beg trouble here by triggering too much sadness about letting this stuff go, but it is important to honor what was good in the relationship. If you don't acknowledge the good things, they will actually haunt you in your conscious thoughts and dreams. In fact, you'll create an argument in your own head. You'll try to get rid of his memory by turning him into a complete villain, but your brain will then be compelled to remind you of all the happy stuff you truly did share.

So again, don't resist this. Instead, go with it, but all the while remind yourself that the bad outweighed the good and that's why you're moving on. Of course, if the chump you've dumped has been a complete bastard, then you can simply pass on this exercise altogether. But if you did share some good times beyond the initial peacock phase, you need to give the positive memories some credit and store them in a safe place so they don't dominate your current mission of ending the pining, fantasizing, and romanticizing.

You need to create a memory box, a place where you will store all the memorabilia worth saving. I suggest you literally create a box and put inside photos, trinkets, greeting cards, love notes, the extra-large T-shirt you slept in that was his, and anything else that makes you say, "Oooooh, he was soooooo sweet!" You might also add a written description of your favorite memories. After all, maybe he was wonderful in these moments. But a healthy relationship can't be based on a few happy times. The grander picture needs to be predominantly positive and supportive.

You can do this exercise one of two ways. You can put everything left over from him inspiring any memory—positive, neutral, or negative—in the box, or you can create several boxes with each one separating the good from the bad, and even from the neutral. Granted, this will most likely be a painful exercise and one you might want to avoid. But I highly recommend you walk through your emotions. Play some music, have a friend help you, or do it just a bit at a time—just do it! You're not going to do anything with the box except put it in a place outside of your main focus. You can put it in a storage unit, up far out of your reach in a closet or garage, or better yet at a trusted friend's or family member's house. Later, after you've completed the Dump That Chump program and are feeling much stronger, you can revisit the box and decide what you'll do with all the stuff, but for now you just need to get it out of your reach.

When you're going through the tangible evidence of him, do keep out one photo, either of the two of you or just of him. Then get out some markers or a black pen and draw all over his face and body, creating the ugliest image of him you can. Keep this marked-up photo with you at all times, and when you're having a flash memory pull it out and remember him in this way. Though he doesn't physically look like how you've drawn him, this will help remind you of how you felt around him, which I'm sure wasn't very good.

Redefining You

Whenever you think of yourself in the context of the chump, you've probably got a mental picture of yourself as pathetic, broken, and unwanted. Or you become overwhelmed with anger, maybe even rage. And then you see yourself as a villain. Neither picture gives you any warm fuzzies. Though hopefully these negative images are beginning to fade and become more positive from the work you did with the last step on transforming self-downers to self-uppers, you're probably still in a slump. So you must actively create a new self-image.

Trina, a thirty-five-year-old woman with an eight-year-old son from a previous marriage, had reentered the dating world after having licked her wounds following a divorce two years prior. She'd done what many women are coached to do. She stayed away from relationships for several months so as to prevent the rebound syndrome. She had gotten on with her life, was no longer feeling like a loser after her failed marriage, and was ready to hit the singles scene once again. "This time around I'll never give my heart away again. I'll just play around and have some fun." But as is true for most women, "sport-dating" doesn't usually work out so well. And it proved to be a disaster for Trina.

Trina joined every online dating service and went to all kinds of singles events. She was on a mission to date a lot without becoming too attached. Of course, she was operating from a false self-image. In other words, deep in her heart she wanted to fall in love again and have a lifelong mate. But she had developed a protective wall, trying to keep up a façade of not really wanting a meaningful relationship.

The whole charade blew up in her face when she started dating David. With David, she acted as if she were a totally self-sufficient woman who needed nothing from anyone. And the relationship would have been perfect had it been true, since David really only wanted a weekly companion for a night of fun and casual sex. He didn't want any commitments or the responsibilities of a relationship. But Trina fell for him, and then she was stuck. In this case, David really wasn't a chump since he had always been honest with her. In fact, she was more the chumplike one, since she'd presented an inauthentic picture of herself. Their fling ended with a lot of tears and begging. But David was clear he couldn't give Trina what she wanted and he stood his ground when he dumped her.

The lesson for Trina was that she hadn't really done any healing after her divorce that would serve her in another relationship. She'd just put a bandage on a wound rather than truly identifying what had gone wrong in her marriage and dealing with the real issues.

Trina's husband had been very controlling and in her face all the time. She had no breathing room. He was insanely jealous and wanted to know her whereabouts every minute of the day. She felt suffocated with no life of her own. Though she'd been very much in love with him, she couldn't live under such dominance anymore, and she felt her only possibility of happiness would come from a divorce. She also falsely concluded that she needed men in her life who made no claims on her.

Trina provides a great example of women who have pendulum relationships—i.e., relationships where they keep picking the opposite kind of guy from the last one. Controlling guy to no-commitment guy. Or super-passive guy to passionate, aggressive guy. The snake to the weasel. Or the bear to the sloth. These polar opposites are equally unsatisfying.

So as you move out of your fantasies of the chump and into the fantasy of you, be extra careful to create a full picture of what you're looking for and of who you really are. Otherwise, if you haven't learned to integrate a full understanding of what you're looking for in a man, you're liable to end up in the same boat as

Trina. The good news is that Trina came to understand this pattern and, once she recognized it, she was able to start focusing on finding someone with a good balance of connectedness and separateness. And she was also able to put herself out there as the full woman she was.

So it's time to get out that journal again and write out a comprehensive picture of the kind of person you are and the person you'd like to attract. Think of descriptive qualities that really appeal to you, keeping in mind that even the chump may have had some redeemable features that you'd prefer in your next guy.

As you work on your fantasy picture, do strive to go much deeper than the superficial and actually think of ways these qualities are manifested. For instance, if you put on your list that you're generous and seeking the same in someone else, then ask, "What does that really mean to me?" Generosity, like all qualities, can be expressed in multiple ways. Generosity to you may involve donating your time to help others in need where you reap no other reward than good feelings. For someone else, generosity may involve giving away money or material goods and getting a tax write-off. Both have merits, but one style may be more fitting to you than another.

Keep this list handy, as you will add to it and modify it later on as you reach the stage of being ready to get back into the dating world.

The Bead Jar

Rewarding ourselves for achieving our goals creates a positive feedback loop. When we take a step forward and then follow up by acknowledging our achievement, we feel better about our efforts and more motivated to continue on a constructive path. Conversely, if we live in constant judgment of ourselves or focus on how bad we feel, we create a negative feedback loop, feeling shame and lack of motivation to be good to ourselves. If there's ever a time to put a positive feedback loop in motion, it's right now while you're weaning yourself from your attachment to the chump. In fact, it's mandatory to praise yourself for any progress you make toward emotionally saying "Bye-bye, Bozo!" for good.

You can reward your progress in all kinds of ways. Just as animals in training love to hear the sound of your voice giving them praise or a rub on the head, so too do humans like to be acknowledged for doing a good job. So don't skimp on this effort.

Select a glass or plastic jar. Go to some kind of arts and crafts store and purchase a big bag of beads. Pick bright colors and lots of varieties. Every time you have an urge to contact the chump and you successfully resist, you'll drop a bead in the jar. Just noticing the jar becoming fuller each day will continue to give you inspiration to stay on the positive path of leaving him in the dust. But if you desire an even greater reward, you can delineate gifts to yourself for your progress. For instance, for every ten beads you will treat yourself to that new awesome-smelling lotion that's way too expensive, but you just love it and gotta have it. Or you'll put five dollars toward a massage you've been dying for but haven't been able to afford.

Make sure your rewards don't go too far overboard, causing other kinds of problems. Don't put yourself into debt you'll later regret or eat so much junk food you're forced to go on a deprivation diet to drop the five pounds you've just gained unnecessarily. The main theme should be about noticing your progress in order to boost your self-esteem. Giving yourself tangible incentives is just the icing on the cake.

*Quick Recipe Guide
for Step Three*

✦ Schedule in your pining time—with the first segment lasting up to thirty minutes, and each consecutive segment reduced by five-minute increments. Your goal is to have no more than seven pining sessions. Don't worry if you have trouble sticking to this limit, but keep trying to push yourself to not indulge when the memories intrude.

✦ Make a list of your needs versus your preferences. Identify which needs the chump fulfilled, which ones he didn't, and ways that you can fulfill your own needs.

✦ Start your bead jar. Purchase what you need or improvise with stuff you have lying around. Decorate your jar. Keep a journal throughout the day of your successes in not acting on your impulses to reach out for him. Also use the beads for all the moments you were able to employ the stop sign method or some other technique to interrupt the pining. After you've accumulated some beads give yourself what you've promised.

✦ Work on your memory box(es) and then store it (them). Get it out of your sight. You will not revisit the box until your self-esteem has improved. By then you may not even care to ever think about him or the memories again!

✦ Go out and have some fun!

Next, you have a big job ahead of you—getting over mad and sad!

Chapter 8

{ step four }

From Mad and Sad to Glad

Way to go, girl! You've physically removed yourself from your relationship and you've worked hard at putting to rest the tendency to pine and fantasize about the chump. Okay, so you may still be pining now and again. Don't worry! That's to be expected, especially if you had been in a long-term relationship with your chump and/or you had taken a long time to actually recognize that he is a chump. Just keep moving forward.

This chapter includes a number of exercises. Read through all of them first before you decide how to pace yourself. I don't want to give you too much structure since you need to determine which of the feelings you tend to be stuck on. If you're primarily caught in the vicious snare of anger and rage, then you may wish to spend more time on the exercises to release those feelings and less time on dealing with sad feelings. Regardless of how you divide your time, just be sure to do these exercises.

But, before we plunge into mad and sad, do the following

prep exercise. Give yourself the biggest hug you can muster and say these words aloud every day (two or three times a day would be even better) for at least the next week:

I'm doing great, no matter how hard this is. I feel [fill in the blank with the emotions you experience—e.g., mad, sad, afraid, etc.] but there's nothing to be ashamed of for having strong feelings. That's simply a natural by-product of having loved and lost, even if the one I lost should have never been found to begin with. I'll get through these feelings because I have the power to choose to be happy. No one can ever take that away from me!

Don't short-change yourself by skipping these mini affirmation moments. Small doses of nurturing self-attention will ultimately be the substance that fills up what feels like an empty hole inside of you. Whether or not you believe these words right now doesn't really matter. If you practice acts of self-directed kindness over and over again, positive results will take hold. And eventually you will come to believe you're fully worth all the fuss. Indirectly you will create an aura around you that tells others that this is the only energy you will ever allow to be directed toward you again. After all, you can't reasonably expect to draw Mr. Right into your life if you don't continually behave like someone who deserves to have the very best. And nothing can rival self-love!

Next, take a few more moments to do the imagery exercise below. This will help get you ready for the next step's challenge, when you will practice the art of self-soothing.

Get into a super-comfy position. Yes, it can be in your bed with fifteen pillows surrounding you, if that's what it takes. Or if you prefer to be curled up in a ball on your favorite chair, then by all means go there. Don't be hasty. Take your time to really pick the spot that will bring you a sense of peace. This is your program, so fine-tune it to find the way it works best for you. Once you're settled into your spot, try the following exercise.

Step One

Create a picture in your mind of someone you believe to be most representative of a loving, nurturing person. And no, it can't be the chump you just dumped, no matter how loving he may have been in his better moments. If you have a parent who fits this description, then the image of him/her would certainly be ideal. But if you're one among the many of us who didn't grow up with the most comforting parenting, then you'll have to think outside the box. You may picture a grandparent, aunt, uncle, big sister, some other relative, or a friend. Or you might need to create a fantasy of someone who embodies all loving and nurturing qualities, using characters from movies or mothers/fathers whom you've watched interacting with their children at the playground. Regardless, let your mind wander to any image that works for you. And don't judge whatever emerges. Just make sure the image offers warmth and love.

For example, Maggie, a forty-something woman, had very abusive parents. So it would not have been in her best interests to think of either of her parents in this capacity. Tragically, she also didn't have any relatives or significant others who would fit the bill. So she had to find an image outside of her personal experience. Much to her surprise her mind delivered a picture of a round African-American woman (though Maggie herself is Caucasian), who smelled of daisies and spoke with a husky Southern cadence. She'd never met this woman, nor had she ever seen the likes of her. Nevertheless, the image she created brought her the most comfort (probably since the woman she pictured in her mind was the polar opposite of her parents).

On the other hand, Marsha, a twenty-something woman who had experienced a close relationship with her mom, remembered many moments throughout her life when her mother comforted her during times of distress. While her mother lived far away during the "dump the chump" phase of her life, Marsha found she could capture in her mind the essence of her mom's protection.

Depending upon your own background, you will have your own source of what feels nurturing. There's no right answer; just make sure it reflects warmth and tender loving care. You might even use a picture of a pet or a favorite stuffed bear that brought you comfort when you felt most vulnerable. Whatever you come up with, picture it very strongly in your mind. Close your eyes and see the image as clearly as you can. Make it real. Try to smell it and feel it in the room with you as a real presence. Don't worry; no one will think you're crazy. You're doing this privately in your own space, not out in public, and not on your boss's time clock. And in case you're still skeptical, ask yourself, "Is staying with someone who doesn't make me happy any less crazy?" I think not.

Step Two

Keeping your eyes closed, have the mothering/comforting figure you've pictured sitting right by your side holding your hand. Now imagine taking in the strength and courage supplied through this source. Take several deep breaths while you fully embrace this image. This becomes your gas line when your fuel tank feels empty. Getting over a breakup, especially with a chump, takes a lot of energy. So make sure you rely on this image whenever you sense you might be losing your forward momentum.

Step Three

Using a journal, write down five to ten quick one-liners that keep you on a positive track. Some examples are:

+ These feelings are only temporary.
+ This too shall pass.
+ Whatever doesn't kill me will make me stronger.
+ One day I'll be able to think about him (the chump, that is) and I'll wonder what in the world I was ever attracted to.
+ This period of recovery is an opportunity to learn great things about myself.

Be creative. Come up with statements that make *you* feel better. Keep these within close reach, and read and say them aloud several times a day. But whatever you do, refrain from any form of self-pity. This loss is not a bad thing. You may be hurting for now, but keep in mind that many good decisions take awhile to reveal their rewards. Now let's tackle the mad and sad feelings.

I'm So Mad

I'm addressing mad before sad, not because there is a right order to dealing with feelings, but because my experience has taught me that many people fortify themselves with anger in order to avoid other feelings like sadness, fear, and hurt. And mad initially gives many women a sense of empowerment to actually make the break. So mad tends to precede the sad. (Of course, if this doesn't fit you, please feel free to read these sections in the reverse order or skip them altogether.)

While feeling mad certainly provides a sense of strength and can help propel you out of a bad relationship, if it lingers on once you've removed yourself then it has overstayed its purpose. In fact, spending even one second invested in the emotion of anger when you're not in the face of your offender is like repeatedly shooting yourself in the foot and waiting for the other guy to say "ouch." It just doesn't make any sense. But this is very hard to comprehend while you're in the throes of your fury. So let's look more closely at the purpose of anger and how to get rid of it.

Many would consider anger to be an emotion just like sad or glad. And in some ways it is. However, more often than not anger is actually a secondary or cover-up emotion, i.e., a feeling that camouflages another. That doesn't mean your anger isn't real, just that more often than not it serves as a defense mechanism rather than as a true emotion.

Anger clearly has some survival value. And when we perceive our well-being or even our values and integrity to be threatened, anger serves as an appropriate and useful emotion. Just as fear mobilizes us into a fight-or-flight reaction when we are faced with a true danger, anger gives us energy to either move away from or stand up to someone who offends us. Hence, it's totally normal to be angry at a chump. After all, most likely he repeatedly violated your boundaries and/or disregarded your needs. He may have even shamed you for simply expecting the basics—love, attention, kindness, support. He wasn't there for you when you needed him and he probably made you think of yourself as too darn needy. He most likely pegged you as the high-maintenance one in the relationship, even though all you asked of him was to love you and care about you. So if getting mad helped you come to recognize the injustice in the relationship and helped mobilize you to get out, then I'm all for it.

But remember that you are now out of the relationship. So don't give him any more power over your emotions than you already have. You're in charge of how you feel. And no one, not even the chump, can make you feel any particular way. You are solely in charge of your emotions.

Unfortunately, many women who've been seduced by chumps

stay mad far longer than is of any value to their actually moving forward. Once you're out of the relationship, mad loses all value and actually becomes counterproductive to your purpose of detaching. In fact, being mad indicates just as much attachment as does being in love. And since your goal is to move on, the last thing you want to encourage is anything that still keeps you connected. Once you stop personalizing what he's done to you and instead frame his behavior as an indicator of who he is, then you can fully separate and maybe even feel sorry for him.

Okay, so now you understand that mad is no longer serving a purpose. "But how do I get rid of it?" you may be asking. The good news is that simply by accepting your anger as useless, you've already created an opening to dispense with it. Now, to fully eliminate its toxicity you must truly practice the following exercise at least once. But feel free to go through it as many times as it takes until your anger disappears.

By the way, I know it can be very tedious to do these exercises, especially when you also have all of your other responsibilities to attend to. But keep in mind that you have spent inordinate amounts of time dwelling on a sour relationship and obsessing about how to get an unworthy guy to love and appreciate you, to no avail. So whatever time you're spending on these exercises will more than likely not even come close to what you've already wasted by ruminating about how you can get your ex to finally adore you or how you wouldn't be without him "if only I had . . ." (Be realistic. You've already tried everything to make it work—he's not going to change!) Plus, doing these exercises will actually yield a very desirable effect—i.e., help you feel better—whereas continually trying to get dust to turn to gold will just make you all dirty, with no reward. So keep reminding yourself that you must continually practice these self-help actions in order to get over him.

Dump That Chump!

Five Steps to Release Your Anger

Step One

Today is your lucky day! You get to spend all of your free time (make some if you don't have any) totally trashing your ex in your fantasy. The operative word here is *fantasy*. You do not have permission to act on any vengeful thoughts, no matter how insignificant you think the action might be. I repeat, you cannot in any way make your fantasies realities. (You don't want to go to jail. And you won't feel good about yourself if you act in ways that make you also qualify as a chump, or worse yet, as a criminal.) But as long as you don't go outside the realm of your imagination, you can go anywhere you like.

Jenny had a particularly fulfilling moment when she allowed her mind to picture Matthew, the chump she dumped, getting fired from his job, eating out of trash bins, and never being able to get another date. She pictured him alone in his apartment, eating ice cream out of a big tub, getting fat, and smelling bad from lack of personal hygiene. (Yeah, that's what she was doing every night for three weeks following their last fight. But in her fantasy, he never gets out of that mode, yet she rises high above it.)

Sarah took particular delight in picturing Robert getting dumped by the girl he opted to share his bed with when Sarah was out of town one weekend. Sarah knew he'd hook up with the other woman as soon as Sarah was out of the picture. Naturally she wanted him to feel the same way she felt when he had cheated on her.

Marcy created quite an elaborate picture of revenge. I won't go into all the gory details, but suffice it to say it involved an apparatus that would cause quite a bit of pain to certain unmentionable body parts.

Don't worry. Imagining vengeance doesn't make you a bad person. We all have sadistic fantasies. After all, it's normal to want to fight back when you perceive you've been wronged or treated badly. Just watch young children interact for a little while—one grabs the other's toy and the other one smashes her on the head impulsively. However, while we're deeply programmed with "an eye for an eye, a tooth for a tooth" level of morality, it's not okay to get this kind of revenge. And clearly we have other options. As long as we keep these impulses confined to fantasy expression, then no harm, no foul. So carry on!

To make this exercise even more cathartic (i.e., helpful to releasing pent-up anger), write out your fantasy of revenge. Read it aloud and give yourself full permission to really feel the anger.

Step Two

Make an extensive list of everything the chump did or said during the course of your relationship that hurt or disrespected you. Don't bother with minor irritations or insults that would be a by-product of any intimate relationship—just the ones that reflect his chumpiness, like breaking promises, repeatedly not showing up to important family events because he preferred playing poker with the guys to spending time with people who are important to you, choosing a boys' night out on your birthday and telling you that you were overreacting when you said you were hurt.

Next, take your list and examine it very closely for any items you've included where in fact you were involved in creating your own misery. I'm not saying you should ever be responsible for his bad behavior, but let's face it: we are not always immune from stirring up trouble. For instance, if he stopped calling you just to say hi because you badgered him with a list of complaints every time he thought to check in, then you need to look at your own role. In those kinds of scenarios, both people played a part in the dysfunction.

Pamela, an extraordinarily creative and intelligent designer, didn't do so well in the intimacy realm, having repeated difficulties in relationships with men. Having come from a very neglectful, at times abusive, background, she was quite familiar with being treated badly. It's as though she wore a sign that said "Welcome All Chumps, Good Guys Needn't Apply" when searching for a new relationship. Then, once in a relationship, Pamela would never dare say what she wanted or needed from her partner; rather, she allowed herself to be treated like a doormat. Then she'd seethe with resentment, but she wouldn't express her dissatisfaction for fear of being dumped. This is not to say that the guys she committed to weren't actual chumps; many of them definitely fit the bill. But there was no real way to know what would have been possible for at least some of her relationships had she been more vocal.

Once Pamela accepted that her fears and resulting passivity contributed to her being treated badly, she became far more empowered in her relationships and much more selective. She recognized the futility of being angry and hurt, waiting for someone to change who had no interest in being different. She learned to speak up. And if she didn't get results, she enlisted her courage to move on without wasting a whole lot of tears on someone who wasn't willing to build healthy intimacy.

By taking ownership of your part (not blame, just accountability), your anger will dissipate. In many cases you will look back at incidents and call it a wash. Sometimes he was in the wrong, sometimes you. You don't have to be angry at yourself and you don't have to be angry at him. Those items can then be removed from the list.

Step Three

For the remaining items on your list, indulge yourself for a moment or two to feel the full extent of your anger concerning the things he did to you that truly reflected chumpy behavior. Then picture a big trash bin in between the two of you. Imagine tossing each and every one of those old hurts into the bin and then putting the lid on the can. Tell him to take his own trash out of your yard, then put up a "No Trespassing" sign. Please don't confront him in person. More than likely he won't accept responsibility and you'll just feel bad all over again. (Remember those are some of the key features of qualifying as a chump—a lack of accountability for wrongdoings and a failure to change hurtful behavior.) But do give yourself the gift of getting rid of the hurt you've been carrying and the anger surrounding it. After all, as long as you're out of his line of fire, there's no reason to be mad anymore.

Step Four

Next, you need to adopt healthy beliefs about your former relationship. Below is a list of core beliefs. By embracing each of them wholeheartedly you will ultimately cut off the energy sources fueling your anger. Although some of these may seem clichéd, overly simplified, or things your mother told you, they still have value and deserve to be incorporated into your recipe for moving forward. Practice saying these aloud several times a day until they actually resonate!

+ I'm better off without him.
+ I can't erase what's happened, but I can certainly learn from it.

✦ This relationship has taught me more about what I don't want in a mate.

✦ Letting go of my anger will free me to feel happy.

✦ I can only find Mr. Right when I'm fully free of Mr. Wrong.

Step Five

Last but not least you must also adopt new beliefs about relationships in general in order to prevent sabotaging the romance you yearn for. If we stay angry at our former lovers we will inevitably carry that energy into our future relationships. We'll be guarded and protective, expecting to be mistreated even when there's no evidence of any chumpy behavior in a new suitor. Or we'll be likely to think of ourselves as victims and then become magnets for those who prey on the vulnerable. We simply must get rid of any remnants of toxic energy. After all, who wants to be around an angry person?

By incorporating the tenets listed below into your relationship mindset, you'll be far better equipped to pick better the next time around.

✦ I have control only over my own reactions, feelings, and thoughts. I can't control another person. Though my lover has an influence on how I feel, he can't *make* me feel any particular way.

✦ I must have reasonable expectations. And it is my responsibility to take care of myself when my partner doesn't meet them. If he repeatedly fails after having agreed to certain standards and I choose to stay anyway, then I can't hold him responsible for my choice.

✦ Contrary to popular belief, I am not better off when I express my anger. Actually, I'm better off not getting angry to begin with by creating relationships with people who respect me. Sure, I'll continue to encounter mild annoyances and irritations, but if I find that I am chronically angry, most likely I'm either letting things get to me more than I should, I'm counting too much on someone else to make me happy, or I'm with a chump and should get out.

I'm So Sad

There's nothing wrong with feeling sad. Of course you feel a sense of loss when a relationship ends. Chump or not, you love(d) the guy. But as with anger, it's important to recognize that you have a choice about whether to continue to feel sad or to move on.

Feelings are directly linked to our perceptions. If we believe we hold something of great value and we lose it, we're likely to experience strong feelings of sadness and loss. For instance, if your best friend moves across the country and you totally cherished her friendship, it's very fitting that you would suffer upon her departure, missing the close contact you've shared over the years. But what if this same "friend" was actually a back-stabbing, gossiping, judgmental bitch, whom you had only stayed in touch with because you'd grown up together and felt a sense of obligation to maintain the illusion of closeness? Would you still feel sad upon hearing the news of her big move? My guess is you wouldn't. Rather, you'd probably be glad.

Or picture this: Your coworker gets a promotion that involves a great deal more work than each of your positions currently requires. If you were coveting the new position, then your coworker getting picked over you might stir up feelings of bitterness, envy, or anger. But what if you're looking to downsize your life and take more time off to travel and get to know yourself better? Well, then you'd likely feel glad for your coworker. You might even be relieved that you don't have to face the difficulty of having to turn down the promotion.

As you can see by the examples above, although some reactions are common to certain situations, we don't have universally determined responses to many events. What makes me feel sad may trigger a happy emotion for you and vice versa. It's all in how we look at things. While humans will most likely feel fear if their lives are threatened and sad if they lose a loved one to death, our feelings are still generated by our subjective perceptions. The emotions we experience depend on the meaning an event has for us. True, while we'll find many other people who will share our experience, there's no absolute right way to feel about any given circumstance. For instance, rejection doesn't always make us feel bad, nor does acceptance necessarily breed good feelings. It's all in whether you perceive something as valuable or not. Also, sometimes we believe we *should* feel a certain way about something—so we distort our perception of what really happened. Then we're not even responding to reality. Don't get caught in this trap. And please know that you have full control over how you choose to perceive a situation.

Now, returning to your breakup with the chump. It may be hard for you to imagine this, but you don't actually have to feel sad at all about this breakup. In fact, once you reframe what you've lost as not having had a great deal of value in the first place, it won't even make sense to feel sad. Sure you might still be missing him. After all, you were most likely very attached to him despite his chronically appalling behavior, and you were hopeful the relationship would have somehow worked itself out. But if you view the breakup as a gain rather than a loss, you can let go of your sadness. Why? Because now you've freed up time and energy to find the real deal.

Consider this hypothetical situation: What if you find a shiny gem while you're taking a walk and you believe it's a diamond? Wow! You've scored. But, uh-oh, you drop it in the gutter. Darn right you're going to be pissed, maybe even deeply sad for a while. But what if that gem had turned out to be a synthetic, having virtually no value? How long would you mourn that loss?

Taylor, a truly adorable and charming young woman, came to my office in a state of utter distress. She'd been in love with Kirk, a not so adorable, certainly not at all charming guy in his mid-thirties. Kirk had proposed to Taylor on two occasions, and both times he reneged on his offer. This in and of itself didn't qualify him as a chump. Rather, what earned him his title was that he wouldn't deal with his ambivalence, kept blaming Taylor for his waffling even though she hadn't changed her behavior a bit, and kept sabotaging the relationship by going to strip clubs with his friends, extending his business trips with extra days of hanging out to relax instead of spending time with her, and "forgetting" about important events he had agreed to attend with her. Plus, when he did change his plans, he wouldn't tell her until he had already screwed up her schedule.

By the time Taylor sought my help, she was a mess. Her stomach was continually in knots and she couldn't sleep, let alone concentrate at work. She had tried several times to break up with him, but he would woo her back into his lair, making insincere promises to "do right by her" if she would only give him another chance. She would continually get seduced by his words, dismissing his repeated acts of disrespect. She later discovered that once, while he had called her to profess his undying love, he was actually making reservations for a weekend getaway with his friends. These so-called buddies were going to set him up for a weekend of sex with another woman!

Shortly into our work together, Taylor found the inner strength to finally make the break. She gave Kirk the boot, and for a while she felt really good. She knew she was standing up for herself in a healthy way and she truly longed for a more gratifying relationship. Of course, as is to be expected, within a few days Taylor became flooded with memories of Kirk, seeing him in a purely glossy form. It was as though someone had gone into her brain, erased every memory of the times when she had felt so much pain, and replaced these with airbrushed photos. Because her mind played these tricks on her, she became overcome by feelings of sadness and loss, actually believing that she'd made a mistake in getting rid of the bum.

I felt so bad for Taylor. I wanted to shelter her from her sorrow and protect her from further harm. But I didn't want to indulge her self-pity. It was clear to me that she would be far better off without Kirk. But at that moment all she could envision was a future of loneliness and total despair. Getting her to see the light was going to take a lot of work.

Fortunately, once Taylor embraced the idea that she was ultimately in charge of her own feelings, we were able to find the true photo negatives of her relationship and get rid of the airbrushed prints. And Taylor was finally able to see Kirk in a more realistic light, dispensing her illusions of his greatness. In doing so, she became free to let go of her sadness and move on to a happier state of being.

You can too! How do you get from sad to glad? You have to put your relationship in its true perspective, eliminate self-criticisms, accept both the good and the bad of the relationship, and focus on the present moment. Do the following four exercises.

Step One

Evaluate the truth of your relationship. Pull your head out of the sand in case you've been stuck there and see the whole picture. There's got to be a good reason for dumping your chump. You got fed up. Don't lose your momentum now. Whatever doubts you're having are probably coming from insecurities in you that cause you to cling to whatever you can. You've accepted crumbs for far too long. You need to set your sights on having the whole loaf. (Okay, so if you're counting carbs, pick another metaphor.) Seriously, there's a good chance you're feeling more sad about not being part of a couple than about having really lost something of value. And understandably you're not yet that keen on the idea of your single status, possibly fearing that you'll never find anyone better. You must acknowledge that your relationship mostly sucked or you wouldn't be in this position.

Step Two

Don't get bogged down by self-criticism. Even if you really believe he wasn't such a chump after all, keep in mind that love shouldn't be so tough. Your chemistry, however intense it might have been, also caused you a great deal of grief. His behavior didn't bring out the best in you. It wasn't a good match. So stop shaming yourself. Instead, give yourself a pat on the back for having had such stamina and endurance and having given the relationship your all. Take every precaution not to make the same mistakes again. You must make a firm commitment to yourself that you will stop going to a convenience store for groceries.

Step Three

Make a list of everything you've gained and learned from the relationship. If your list is short, that's fine. But you must come up with at least three things. Aside from completely abusive relationships, every bond has some redeeming aspects. In fact, very rarely do we pick so badly that we want a new partner who is the polar opposite to the chump. By recognizing the positive aspects of the relationship, you'll be less likely to believe that you wasted all your time (yet another burden that keeps the sad feelings alive). Plus, this list will be useful later while you're prepping yourself for the dating scene, helping you increase your chances of finding someone else.

Samantha discovered many wonderful things about herself during her mourning phase. She recognized how sensitive she is and how much she requires a guy who will cherish this about her. She learned that she enjoys challenges, and is unlikely to be drawn to an easy course. For instance, rather than trying to get a completely immature guy to change his ways because of his love for her (a very futile endeavor, she learned), she realized she could experience intensity through activities with a mate with whom she could reasonably expect some success. With her new insights, Samantha took up rock-climbing instead of deadbeat-climbing.

Step Four

Focus on the present instead of jumping into the future. And don't turn to self-destructive means to make yourself feel better. Right now, the only thing you have any control over is your own feelings and reactions. Now is not the time to find someone new to fill up your empty void. Your immediate focus needs to stay with moving through your sadness and inviting in gladness. Tell yourself your feelings are not your enemies. They won't kill you or harm you in any way. And the better you get at allowing your feelings to pass through you, the stronger you'll be.

Spend some time journaling and releasing your sadness. Give your feelings ample airtime, but don't let them steal the mike.

Keep reminding yourself that you can let go of your sadness anytime you wish. You hold the key to unlocking your joy.

The Power of Distraction and Doing the Opposite

Since the rest of the world won't likely grant you immunity from your daily responsibilities simply because you believe your heart is broken, it's good to have a few extra tools at hand when you're required to function. My favorite ones are distraction and doing the opposite of what you're used to doing. You can use these methods anytime you're having difficulty coping with painful feelings, not only while working through this step. But just make sure you do the work of moving through your emotions and don't rely exclusively on these tools as a way of avoiding it.

The Power of Distraction: We distract ourselves all the time when we have too much stress, feel burned out, or are just having a bad day at work. We crash in front of the television, watching mindless programming. Or we daydream about a trip to Hawaii we're not likely to take anytime soon, but it's a heck of a lot better than thinking about the fight we just had with our mother. So why not steer clear of thinking about the train wreck you've recently endured. After all, you can't heal everything in one day. You deserve a break.

Although learning to self-soothe does the best job of taking the pain away from something that hurts us, we won't always have the time or the right circumstances to give ourselves exactly what we need. Hence, engaging in distraction can buy you some time and get you through some difficult moments.

Distraction only becomes avoidance or procrastination if you don't regularly revisit the work you must ultimately do to free yourself of the toxic hold this former love has had over you. So go ahead—live a little. Find some activities you enjoy that keep your mind off the chump. Go to the movies with a good friend, take a tennis lesson with a cute instructor, or listen to the music you used to enjoy in childhood, long before you ever met your ex. Spend some money you were saving for that weekend getaway you had expected to take with him but in hindsight realize would never have really happened anyway. Try out an exotic recipe and invite friends over to eat a fun dinner. (Of course, you might consider having delivery ser vice available as backup, should the meal taste like cardboard!) Whatever you choose, pick something you didn't routinely do with the chump. Otherwise you'll just set yourself up to reminisce about past times. And that's the last energy you want to re-create at this moment. Later you will conquer the challenge of reengaging in the routines you once shared with him, if you so desire.

Doing the Opposite: People develop predictable habitual patterns of responding to many daily activities because these behaviors have become linked to a particular stimulus. For instance, smokers often feel the urge to smoke when they encounter the smell of coffee, if they have come to associate drinking coffee (stimulus) with having a smoke (response). The aroma of the coffee alone can trigger the urge to smoke.

If you'd developed routines with your partner you're certainly going to feel a void if you continue to do the same things without him. Not forever, but certainly while you're in the mourning phase. You might have come to associate some of your routines with your ex and be more inclined to romanticize him while engaged in these activities. In other words, participating in the activity you used to do as a couple may trigger memories of the relationship, and hence the feelings that went along with them. This can be a good thing when you're involved with Mr. Right. If you watch a movie you and he both love while he's away on a business trip, this may help you feel closer to him, missing him a little less. But the reverse can happen when you try to engage in routines linked to memories of a chump. Rather than conjuring up good feelings, you're likely instead to trigger either loss and sadness or anger and betrayal—none of which is desirable. To prevent or combat the bad feelings, try doing the opposite of what you used to do while involved with your former chump. That way you can create new associations and responses to new experiences—ideally much happier ones.

Jenny and Matthew went to their favorite Italian restaurant on Friday nights, usually sharing a pasta dish and a bowl of soup. Initially she recalled this event fondly, failing to remember the many times they had spent the evening fighting. But later she remembered the anguish she endured on many of these occasions. Often he would make plans to be without her on Saturday night, not informing her until that morning. Yet he was the guy who had originally pushed for a more committed relationship where they would spend more time as a couple.

After finally summoning the courage to dump Matthew, Jenny still felt compelled to go back to this restaurant on Friday nights, hoping to rekindle good feelings. But what she quickly recognized was that this only made her feel unbearable sadness, and her being there certainly wasn't going to bring Matthew back (not that she even really wanted him back). Jenny had become used to this shared activity, associating Friday night romance with this restaurant. And while she had to ultimately learn to relinquish this place as "theirs" and neutralize it so that it didn't have any power over her, temporarily she was better off not going there at all and instead choosing a very different activity to help break the association to Matthew. Jenny opted to join a running club, which met at a track each week around the same time she would have been dining with Matthew. Then, once she was fully over Matthew, she was able to revisit this restaurant and enjoy the delectable entrees without missing him. (Later you will learn how to reclaim all your old spots and activities.)

Think of a few things you can do that are totally foreign to your former relationship. When you find yourself getting really sad about your breakup, put these into action. I know this can be difficult. But remember: your ultimate goal is to get over him and become ready to create a successful relationship. If that means narrowing your world a bit on the front end to save a lot of pain in the interim, I think it's well worth the sacrifice. Plus, like Jenny, you'll soon be able to revisit all your former experiences with a new healthier attitude.

Hello, Glad

Come on, admit it! There's some relief in saying good-bye to mad and sad. I know you're not feeling happy every moment. That wouldn't be natural. But it's about time you invite in glad and recognize it when it's present.

To accentuate your happy feelings, please create a separate journal where you jot down each and every moment where you experience joy. You don't have to be euphoric for it to count. Although it's tempting to wallow in self-pity, resist the pull. Remember, you haven't lost a precious gem; you've dumped a chump. Embrace your strength and courage, and SMILE!

Quick Recipe Guide for Step Four

✦ Practice the art of distraction and breaking old habits every chance you get when you need to keep yourself focused on your daily responsibilities. And don't forget some of the other tools from earlier chapters, like the Stop Sign. These can always come in handy in a pinch.

✦ Spend every moment you have during the day outside of work or other mandatory responsibilities practicing the soothing exercise at the beginning of this chapter. You cannot do this too much. Of course, it's not possible to do this with such intensity everyday and also have a life, but for now, do it a lot!

✦ Go through all the exercises in this chapter to help eliminate your anger.

✦ Go through the sad-busting exercises.

✦ Doctor's orders: Go out and have a good time. Do something you've been wanting to do but haven't had the time. Plan a really fun day, go see a movie, or go to a comedy club. You need to laugh. Laughter begets laughter. And even the act of smiling can improve your mood, since smiling triggers the release of happy chemicals in the brain. So plaster that smile on your face, think of happy things, and do something that brings you joy!

Chapter 9

{ step five }

Givin' Yourself Some Lovin'

Please pause for a moment and acknowledge your progress thus far. You've arrived at the hump! It's like Wednesday in the workplace. Pretty soon you'll be saying, "Thank God it's Friday."

This is the time when it's particularly important to stay on track. You've come so far, getting through some enormous challenges. Now the journey should become easier and easier. We're done focusing on the chump. He's old news now. I know you may still picture him on your mind's front page from time to time. But you don't have to give this image any power. Instead, keep reminding yourself that the chump no longer deserves headline coverage!

To move forward, you must now shift all of your attention to building your inner resources. Through your own self-care, you'll become primed to search for and attract Mr. Right. And that requires learning the art of self-lovin'. While you may initially wish to trivialize the importance of self-lovin', this step ranks as one of the most critical aspects to feeling better, once and for all, and to staying in good spirits, regardless of what's going on in your life at any given time. Knowing how to self-soothe quickly catapults you toward creating your own happiness, whether single or in a relationship.

Mind you, I know this may prove to be a very big challenge. Far too many of us haven't received the sort of parenting required to become good self-soothers. Maybe your folks were too busy, too preoccupied, or too naïve to understand the importance of self-soothing, let alone to dedicate time to teaching it. Or maybe a sibling hogged all the attention, leaving little left over for your needs. Or maybe your parents divorced, and dealing with financial strain took precedence over helping you learn to nurture yourself. These or any other number of circumstances may have put the art of self-soothing last on the list.

Sure, many of us learned how to care for ourselves on a physical level. We learned how to brush our teeth and hair, take a shower, and use deodorant. We shave or wax our legs and underarms. We pluck our eyebrows and apply the latest and greatest mascara, hoping our plusher eyelashes will draw more attention to us. Many women spend hundreds, even thousands, of dollars per year on beauty products, hair dye, and waxing salons. Some even resort to plastic surgery, believing that bigger boobs or a smaller nose will compensate for a poor self-image. Regardless of how much attention we may pay to our outer shell, most of us got short-changed when it comes to understanding how to provide enough attention to our inner emotional life.

You don't have to have been badly abused or neglected to fall short on adequate self-lovin.' Many women who've been in a relationship with a chump experienced childhoods with well-intentioned caregivers. In fact, more often than not, we haven't learned to love ourselves because our own parents never learned positive self-care, let alone how to model self-care to their children. It was like the blind leading the blind. Or for those who had it really bad (those who were abused, neglected, or abandoned), not only are you ill-equipped to soothe yourself, you might even be prone to something far worse than the absence of self-care. You might go the other way entirely, practicing self-destruction. But the great news is that it's never too late to reverse destructive or unhealthy patterns.

Because the art of self-soothing rarely gets adequately passed down from our caregivers, first and foremost we need to teach ourselves from the ground up by learning to recognize our own needs and how to meet them. Second, we need to develop realistic expectations of others. More often than not, women grow up believing that their lover's job is to sweep them off their feet and make them happy. To make matters worse, many women, particularly those who've been involved with one or more chumps, have very little positive self-worth. They've become dependent on a man for a 24/7 IV of TLC (tender loving care). Should the IV be removed or should it contain a drip of something toxic, many women have no idea how to find ample nourishment.

Thinking you need a man to fill up your holes and make you happy is just about the worst premise you can have if you want a long-lasting and *loving* intimate relationship. Expecting someone else to make you whole creates a formula for failure. I know this sounds clichéd, but I have to say it anyway. No one, and I mean no one, should ever carry the burden of making you happy. Sure, your beau, hubby, lover, whoever should be a source of support and should provide love, but he should not be your life-preserver or oxygen mask. You must become the supplier of your own well-being and contentment. But obviously you need to know how.

And once you understand how to give yourself lovin', you'll soon discover how the quality of your life and your relationships is intimately tied to your ability to self-soothe.

The Foundations of Self-Lovin'

I won't go into too much detail about why you may have trouble in this area, but I think at least a little bit of understanding helps build compassion, a very necessary ingredient for successful self-soothing.

The foundations of self-lovin' begin in infancy, when your body's needs dominate your experiences. It's pretty simple actually. Our innate goals are to survive and to be comfortable. Of course, as we develop, we become a lot more complicated, but our basic needs never change. At the core, we all need food, water, rest, and shelter and/or clothing for temperature regulation. If our caregivers meet these needs, then we have room to feel the higher-order needs such as love, nurturance, sense of belonging, self-esteem, stimulation, play, spiritual growth, and exploration of our environment. All of our needs are important, but at any point when our basic core needs are jeopardized, our awareness pulls us in this direction.

At first, we're entirely dependent on others to supply us with what we need. When our homeostasis (fancy word for inner balance) goes out of whack, we let our caregivers know by belting out a tune akin to a raging siren or some other nasty sound. Anyone in earshot has to pay attention, or we howl even louder. If our caregivers adequately attend to us, by figuring out what we need and supplying it, we get back in balance. This process provides the basis for self-soothing. Ideally, as we grow up we learn to rely more and more on our own selves to provide comfort and soothing.

Children resort to all kinds of ways to comfort themselves—through thumb-sucking, sniffing a favorite blanket, or rubbing a soft teddy bear against a cheek. All of these mechanisms create a comfort level and help a child feel safe in the world. As we get older, we learn other ways to self-soothe. Once we've reached adulthood, if all went well, we're able to identify our need, scan ourselves and the environment for the best fit to meet the need, and then take action toward fulfillment. If I'm hungry, I eat. If I'm thirsty, I drink. If I'm tired, I rest. If I'm bored, I move toward an activity that's more stimulating. If I'm lonely, I comfort myself and see whether my friends are available to keep me company.

Sounds easy, doesn't it? But as you can see, our ability to learn this process often gets totally screwed up along the way, leaving us ill-equipped to handle this very important job. Some people have no idea what they need at any given moment, having become completely disconnected from their own selves. Others know what their needs are, but they feel ashamed for having them and so they repress or deny the needs. Others go to all the wrong people and places to meet their needs, not knowing that they themselves have the supplies within them.

Caroline's mom had loads of issues regarding what other people thought of her. When Caroline was a little girl, she sucked her thumb whenever she felt anxious or needed some comfort. No doubt she would have weaned herself off her thumb by the time she went to school, but Caroline's mom was mortified at the thought that her child would look like a baby to others. She feared that her daughter's thumb-sucking at age five reflected poorly on her mothering abilities.

Sadly for Caroline, her mom kept pulling her thumb out of her mouth, shaming her with statements like "Big girls don't suck their thumbs. You don't want to be a baby, do you?" While Caroline's mom was trying to help her daughter, she was actually interrupting Caroline's ability to learn to self-soothe. Often her mom would shove a lollypop in Caroline's mouth to avoid the embarrassment she felt while out in public with Caroline. She often appeased her daughter with food instead of comfort. No big surprise that as an adult, Caroline often misread her own needs for emotional soothing as physical hunger. She even had a bout of bulimia in her teens.

In contrast, Lola's parents were overly indulgent with Lola. They couldn't tolerate her being uncomfortable for even a moment. They constantly gave in to her every whim, buying her everything she pointed to and never being able to say no. As an adult, she was in constant search for a guy who would replace Daddy and spoil her. She was bound to end up with a chump at some point since her criteria for a "good man" were all messed up. All she cared about was how much money he made and the fancy places he would take her. Once in the relationship, she would chronically feel unfulfilled because she actually had more needs than she acknowledged, such as a desire for independence. Luckily, before she went on to the next guy, she learned that she needed to figure out what she was really about.

If you have trouble knowing how to self-soothe, don't despair. You can learn how at any age! And once you try it, I'm pretty certain you'll like it.

Self-Lovin' Assessment

Now let's take a look at how skilled you already are in this department. And remember, as always, whatever you discover, don't shame or put yourself down. When we get a clear picture of our vulnerabilities, we can then make choices about how to become stronger. But when we stick our head in the sand, we develop bad habits to compensate for our holes. And these adjustments never sufficiently do the trick of filling us up, let alone get rid of the holes. Go through the checklist below to see where you stand on the continuum of self-lovin'.

When responding to the statements below, use the following rating scale:

0: never   1: rarely   2: sometimes   3: often   4: constantly

__ I eat healthy foods when I'm hungry, rather than grazing on junk or not eating at all.

__ I stop eating when I'm satiated, not stuffed.

__ I drink water or other nourishing liquids when I'm thirsty.

__ I'm aware of my body temperature and dress accordingly (e.g., when I'm cold I put on a sweater or jacket).

__ When I'm tired, I make time to rest.

__ I'm nice and gentle with myself when I make a mistake.

__ I look for ways in which I can improve my mood or help myself feel better when I'm upset about something.

__ I get myself out of destructive situations quickly.

__ I feel responsible for my own happiness in a relationship.

__ I say positive things to myself daily.

__ I live a balanced life of work, rest, and play.

__ I enjoy the activities I choose to participate in, rather than complaining about being bored or feeling like I'm just fulfilling some obligation.

__ I can be happy doing something alone, even though I might prefer others to be with me.

__ I get up and attend to my daily activities even when I'm feeling down.

__ I have control over how I feel about myself.

Givin' Yourself Some Lovin'

___ I expect to be treated with respect and kindness and, when I'm not treated this way, I recognize I have an option to leave.

___ I allow time every day to unwind and get rid of any stress I've absorbed.

___ I think about how I might feel in certain situations before committing to them (e.g., I'll turn down a dinner invitation if I have a really big project to finish at work that requires me to get into the office super-early the next day).

___ I routinely check in with myself about how I'm feeling, and I attend to whether I need to change the way I'm thinking or what I'm doing in order to better meet my needs.

___ I take time out every day to do something I want to do that only benefits me, or at least serves my primary purpose of maintaining or bettering my mental health.

___ I'm attentive to other people's needs and feelings but I don't feel responsible for what other people think and feel. (Unless it's my own child, for whom I do have more responsibility.)

___ I know how to comfort myself when I'm afraid or disappointed.

___ I can quickly get myself back into the present moment when I start dwelling on the future or something I have no immediate control over.

___ Unless there's a true crisis going on, I generally feel at peace in most situations.

___ I like the person I am.

Now add up your score and use the following scale to estimate where you lie on the self-soothing continuum.

0–25: If you scored in this range, you probably have a great deal of difficulty comforting yourself when you feel upset. You may even have trouble taking care of yourself in general, even when you're not in breakup crisis mode. Self-lovin' hasn't been a priority. You probably didn't get a whole lot of emotional goodies from your caregivers in childhood. Hence, you didn't learn how to lovingly parent yourself. Or you may have been overly indulged in childhood, with all of your whims being immediately satisfied, just like Lola. Hence, you were never given the opportunity to embrace the job of parenting yourself. People in this category usually have little awareness of their body and what's going on internally. They feel helpless about where to go once a need surfaces. Fortunately, it's never too late to learn to self-soothe.

Please note that oftentimes the people who score really low on the self-lovin' scale actually have great skills in soothing. Their skills are simply misdirected. While they suck at soothing themselves, when asked how they rate on soothing others, they go off the charts. In other words, they soothe others who are in need, but these same gals have great difficulty turning this energy inward. So if this applies to you, you have an inbred advantage, and you're in better shape than you might think. All you have to do is grasp the energy you already house inside you and redirect at least some of it to your own person.

26–50: If you scored in this range, you certainly have at least a few moments during which you adequately care for yourself. And it's possible you would score even higher if you weren't in the throes of recovering from a breakup. But you still have some work to do since you don't consistently give yourself the kind of self-care necessary to be well-balanced and happy. You may be bitter toward someone from your childhood whom you believe abused or failed you in some significant way. Hence, you might be holding out for someone else to make the repair. But while it would certainly be really nice if the people who wounded us were able to right their wrongs and get us off the hook, most often people don't offer this kind of repair. And waiting around for apologies from others, rather than accepting your own job to take care of yourself, is like cutting off your nose to spite your face. It's time to make self-soothing your number-one priority and stop leaving yourself dependent on others.

51–75: If you scored in this range, you probably fare pretty well, unless life starts throwing you too many curve balls. As long as things move along smoothly, you're okay. But you likely lose some steam when you're stressed out or particularly distraught (as in when you're dumping/have dumped a chump). Understandably you may regress to a more childlike dependent position when you've been beaten down by a bad relationship. Maybe you care for yourself physically but you fall short on the emotional supplies or vice versa. Fortunately, however, you already have what you need for self-soothing. You don't have to start from scratch. You just need to practice applying the methods consistently, particularly at times when your self-esteem has taken a dip.

76–100: This is the scoring range we all hope to achieve, but it's unlikely you're here at this time. But, hey, maybe you have mastered the art of self-soothing throughout the course of your life, and you simply had a momentary loss of consciousness when you hooked up with the chump. It could happen! But it's more likely that you're padding your answers just a bit. Nevertheless, if you did score in this range, check out the individual items where you scored less than a 3 and hone in on developing these areas specifically.

Steps to Becoming a Great Self-Soother

You can become a great self-soother, regardless of your past history. But just in case you're stuck in the blame game, you must let go of holding other people hostage to the mistakes they may have made with you. If you feel deeply wounded, emotionally, you have to do whatever healing work you require so that you can start with a clean slate, knowing that it's your job and no one else's to give yourself love, care, and soothing. While I am entirely empathetic to your suffering, and I wholeheartedly wish that you had been given a solid foundation from the get-go, it will do you no good to harbor resentments or wait for others to make up for whatever was lacking in your development. You need to claim responsibility for your own self-care. Whatever you get from others becomes a bonus, not your lifeline.

To become a great self-soother, you simply have to start practicing right away. All it takes is recognizing your needs from the ground up, developing a broad repertoire of resources to meet your needs, and becoming proactive in fulfilling what you discover.

While I'd love to give you a detailed list of how to soothe all of your needs, to do so would take an entire book in and of itself. And I'd still come up short. But what I have provided are some general tips for how to increase your success at self-care using what I call the NEED arc:

- N: Notice what you need.
- E: Explore both internal and external options to meet the need.
- E: Energize yourself to gratify the need.
- D: Deliver the goods.

Notice what you need.

Obviously you can't meet your needs if you're not even aware that you have any or if you tend to ignore or repress them. So from here on, you must claim that you have needs and be willing to see what they are.

Let's start with recognizing your needs on a physical level. This requires body awareness, which requires paying attention to the signs and signals your body gives you about what you need. People who don't have a clue how to self-soothe often dismiss the multiple cues their bodies provide them on an ongoing basis. Hence, their needs remain unfulfilled.

As I've already mentioned, your body has a built-in capacity to alert you to threats to your survival. If you go too long without eating, your tummy will grumble. If you don't drink enough water, your mouth will become dry, producing less saliva. If you're too hot, you'll start to sweat; if too cold, you'll shiver. You don't have to think about these things; your body does the thinking for you. But oftentimes you do need to take some sort of action in order to satiate the need, like raiding the fridge or gulping down a big bottle of water.

When practicing self-care, it's essential to start with the basics, attending to your core survival needs. Once you've checked in on a physical level, then you can move into the emotional, psychological, and spiritual realms of life. But all the while you have to recheck what your *body* needs. After all, your body serves as your transportation through life. And to have successful intimate relationships, you have to know your body.

When attending to your emotional well-being, you need to know what you're feeling at any given moment. Keep it simple: mad, glad, sad, afraid—or some combo-pack of these emotions. Awareness of our feelings helps determine the actions we may need to take. Certain actions are more fitting to one feeling than to another. For instance, if you're mad you may need to either change your perception or expectations of a situation or remove yourself from whatever stirs up the anger. Conversely, if you feel sad about something, you simply may need to say some gentle words to yourself and allow the feeling to pass through you. If you're afraid of something, you need to assess if there's real danger, or just one imagined in your head.

Though certain feelings will often lead to a particular action, we need to stay flexible and open to many options. What works in one moment may lose its value the next. For instance, sometimes you may wish to be alone while processing your feelings, whereas other times, you may need the comfort of a friend's listening ear.

What are our emotional needs, anyway? Do we all have the same needs in the same quantities? The verdict is still out on these questions, but I can safely say we all need many things to live a fulfilling life, though the degree to which we need these things may vary across time in our own lives and definitely across people. In general, we need love, attention, approval, a sense of belonging, and companionship. We need touch and physical affection. We also need sex, though some would argue that this is just a man-thing. But I beg to differ. When a woman feels good about herself and her body, her sexuality sings to her far more acutely.

When assessing our emotional needs, what's important to remember is that we can meet these needs in multiple ways, often through our own self-care. Remember preferences versus needs? Almost always even if we have a need, we have many options for how to satisfy it. For instance, when we really feel the need for contact with another human being, there's more than one person on earth who can offer supplies. This is particularly good news because that means that we never need a chump. (Okay, it wouldn't surprise me if your mind has created the one and only instance when you would *need* a chump. The "if I were on a desert island" scenario. Okay, I'll grant you this: if you and a chump were the only two people on a desert island, you might end up needing each other. But in that case, I'd first suggest you consider celibacy, masturbation, or a fuzzy leaf against your skin before turning to him for need-gratification! ☺)

We also have many psychological needs (intellectual stimulation, cultural awareness, expression of our thoughts, opinions, and creativity). And as is the case with our physical and emotional needs, the methods we may use to meet them can be as diverse as the different types of flowers that exist. What feels good to me may bore you to tears and vice versa.

We also have spiritual needs. And these are even harder to quantify, especially since values come into play and people have very strong opinions about this area. Nevertheless, this is part of the human experience, even if your course is to reject all spiritual notions. So recognizing your own spiritual needs and moving in the direction of fulfillment is an essential piece of self-lovin'.

Explore both internal and external options to meet the need.

Once you become aware of a particular need, you also become faced with a decision for how to meet it. And appreciating that you usually have many options to meet a need will continue to strengthen your foundation for becoming a good self-care provider. But unfortunately, women who've been with chumps tend to have a limited understanding of the options they have. Namely, they've come to believe that a chump is the only well for water, no matter how dried-up the well is. So you must expand your horizons.

Vanessa's story provides a classic example of someone who

hadn't had any idea how vast her options could be when it came to getting her needs met. After having served what felt like a lifelong sentence hooked up with a chump (though it was actually just five years), Vanessa finally gave Kevin his walking papers. Devastated by the breakup, she came in for counseling. At thirty years old, eager to get married and start a family, Vanessa understood that if she continued on a path with guys like Kevin, she'd be doomed to a life of unhappiness. She wanted an intimate relationship with someone who would treat her well, but she had no idea that her inability to care for herself seriously interfered with her ability to accomplish her love goals.

Vanessa had always looked outside herself for need gratification, and even then her options in her mind were very limited. Of course, this is a good thing if it comes to feeding your physical hunger. You wouldn't want to eat your own finger. In other words, you want to use resources other than yourself. But just like we have choices when we're hungry—eating junk food or something healthier—Vanessa had options other than turning to Kevin to get her emotional needs met.

Though initially Vanessa couldn't see outside the box, she quickly came to understand that Kevin was the equivalent of a fast-food restaurant, which heavily relies on preservatives to make its food taste good—hardly a place for daily consumption if she wanted a healthy body. Basically she realized that Kevin was only nice to her while they were having sex. Any other time, he was a real creep. Though she needed affection and contact, she finally understood that she didn't have to seek it from him. Keeping with the food analogy, Vanessa discovered she didn't have to ingest the MSG in order to get the veggies. She could get her veggies from a more organic source.

So be creative when you have a need. First look to yourself for supplies. If you're not able to meet your own need, run through a checklist of all options available. Always have backup plans just in case you can't get satiated through your primary preferences.

Energize yourself to gratify the need

You understand you have a need, and you have multiple options to meet it. But you won't be satiated unless you know how to rev up your engine so you can get the energy you require to actually take action toward meeting your need.

We can kill our energy for meeting our needs in all sorts of ways. We may distract ourselves too much, minimize the importance of our needs, or convince ourselves that we don't actually have any needs at all. But hey, girl, you have needs, and that is OKAY. Face it. You're human and there's not a thing wrong with you for having needs.

So from today forward, promise yourself that you will embrace your needs and give yourself positive feedback for meeting them. Talk nicely to yourself. Be reassuring and comforting. Assuming you're not endorsing any self-destructive tendencies you've mislabeled as needs, such as overeating, overspending, or locking yourself in your home for days on end with no contact with anyone else, then I encourage you to say something like the following whenever you experience a need. "Okay, I have a need for _____ [fill in the blank]. My needs are normal and healthy, and it's my job to meet them. How can I provide for myself in a healthy, self-caring way?" Accepting your needs as they come and supporting yourself in finding healthy ways to meet them will give you positive energy toward actually taking action.

Deliver the goods.

Meeting our own needs requires more than knowing what they are, how to meet them, and supporting their existence. The process also requires actually implementing your plan. If you decide you need to get some rest and the best way to do it is for you to take a nap, then you must take the nap. Otherwise all your efforts at self-care become wasted. So no matter how bad you might be feeling, get off your butt and do something about it. Don't wait until you're desperate. Take your life back into your own control and actively take steps to make it better every single minute. I guarantee you'll feel better right away if you put a plan into motion.

Quick Recipe Guide for Step Five

✦ Identify the ways in which you are a good self-nurturer and the areas in which you need improvement. Use the assessment tool in this chapter as a guide.

✦ Make a vow to become the number-one provider of your needs. Make a chart of methods you can use as alternatives to meet your own needs when you require external sources.

✦ Practice awareness and fulfillment of your body's physical needs. Be the best parent you can be to your own body.

✦ Practice awareness and fulfillment of your emotional needs.

✦ Practice awareness and fulfillment of your psychological needs.

✦ Practice awareness and fulfillment of your spiritual needs.

✦ Journal extensively about what you've learned.

Chapter 10

{ step six }

Accepting Your Own Screwups

I don't know about you, but I'm not the easiest person to live with. But then again, who is? If we honestly assess ourselves, each of us would admit to being high-maintenance, at least from time to time. Everyone has areas where she can be difficult. So while the chump wins the "most atrocious behavior" award, no doubt you share a role in messing up your love life. And you can't truly move on to another relationship unless you face your own demons head-on. Plus you also have to leave behind all regrets in order to move forward with a clean slate.

I'm sure you've gotten the message by now that it doesn't do you any good to play the shame-blame game: the endlessly destructive cycle of beating yourself up for mistakes, and/or pointing the finger at everyone else for theirs. Instead you have to recognize your own screwups, admit to your shortcomings, and be proactive about making changes in how you approach relationships. For instance, if you discover that you tend to be a doormat with your partner (allowing him to make all the decisions, even when you have strong contrary opinions), you would not improve the situation by focusing solely on how you're being walked all over. You would be wiser to do something proactive. In other words, don't expect him to stop stepping on you just because you tell him you feel mistreated and unappreciated. Instead, you should remove the mat!

Nadine, a twenty-seven-year-old woman, had already been engaged twice. Neither engagement resulted in marriage. Thankfully, prior to tying the knot, she recognized both guys were controlling jerks, continually tightening the noose around her neck as the wedding day approached. She was the one who ended both of these relationships.

While Nadine had a good sense of what these guys were doing to her, she wasn't taking responsibility for what she was doing to herself and to the guys. Though she wasn't being malicious, unbeknownst to her, she'd led both these guys to believe she was a very passive person with no backbone or opinions of her own. In reality, she had a lot to say about a lot of things. They had no idea they were signing up for a relationship with a very strong-willed woman, posing as a dove. As she expressed more and more of her true self, in their own unique ways, these guys became more and more aggressive, trying to get her to be the submissive gal she'd initially presented to them. Not to excuse their behavior, but you can understand that Nadine herself was no innocent bystander.

When Nadine began seriously dating yet another guy, she was about to go down the same road, hiding her true self for fear of being rejected. But Nadine wasn't doing herself, or the new guy, any favors. He was getting a false sense of Nadine's personality, and she was setting herself up, once again, to possibly feel controlled and resentful. She kept thinking she'd meet a guy who would pull her true self out and would never take advantage of her. But until she learned that it was her job to be forthcoming about who she is, she would likely repeat the same disappointments over and over again. Sure, the guys she had left were no great shakes, but hey, she was selling them a crock of lies.

Fortunately, before getting in too deep with guy number three, Nadine came to understand that she'd be far better off embracing her own strong-willed personality and finding someone who would value her strength, not someone who would quell it. Even if she were to be rejected, this wouldn't be so bad since she had finally come to appreciate that she would never be happy with a guy who was intimidated by her. She needed to be with a guy who would cherish her and who would enjoy her gregarious and powerful energy. And, yes, these guys do exist!

Common Myths Women Buy

In order to identify your own screwups and the actions necessary to clean up your act, you must first eliminate any myths you believe, consciously or unconsciously, about being a female. If you hold any negative gender prescriptions, you'll be working against your goal of creating a positive love life. I can't tell you how powerful these myths can be in terms of seriously reducing your chances of capturing Mr. Right.

Clearly, we women have come a long way in terms of earning our rights and increased respect in society. But despite all our progress, we still receive a hefty dose of negative input about what's acceptable behavior for women. These definitions of our roles and behavior can come from parents, teachers, and other influential caregivers, but also largely from the media. (As I'm sure you're well aware, women are not always displayed in the most favorable light in media images. For instance, blondes are often cast as bimbos, especially the well-endowed ones, and heavier women get cast in matronly roles, rather than the sexier ones.)

Whether or not you're aware of the myths we're still being sold, they continue to have an impact. And they most definitely interfere with the ability to have a healthy relationship with a man. Some of the more common myths held by women include:

+ Tone yourself down so you don't outshine the men around you.
+ Keep your true opinions to yourself, especially if your views contradict those of the men around you.
+ Make yourself meek and small so you don't intimidate men, particularly those who are insecure.
+ Male egos are very fragile. Your job is to protect your man from feeling inadequate.
+ Accept your second-class status so you don't disrupt the status quo.

While it's impossible to grow up in today's society without being at least a little bit affected by these myths, I hope you haven't been bombarded by such hogwash! Whatever the level of impact, you must quickly dump all this baloney right along with the chump. Women have every right to their fair and equal share of all of life's offerings, including the right to speak their minds (even if it means disagreeing with others) and the right to be treated with respect. Granted, if we want to have successful relationships, intimate ones or otherwise, we need to be tactful about how we express ourselves. We need to refrain from judging or putting others down and from abusing others. But we absolutely have to value our gender as much as we hold the male specimen in esteem. Otherwise we become walking targets for other chumps to pounce on us.

I don't want you to end up in the same boat again (hooking up with a chump) and I'm certain you don't either. So please take this information very seriously. And don't succumb to any of these misguided rumors about what females should be like. I'm certainly not advocating arrogance or a sense of superiority. But we all deserve a healthy dose of solid self-esteem. So start accepting your fair share!

Just in case you are holding on to any of these fallacies, then you must perform a "mythectomy" (that is, a surgical removal of all undesirable negative messages). Just kidding—there's no real surgery here. But I do want you to purge all this unnecessary negative stuff. You can start by going through these myths once again and identifying which ones you've bought. Also make a list of any other negative messages you've internalized. Put these on paper and burn them. Then solemnly swear to shift your thinking to a positive, self-respecting position.

Identifying Your Own Screwups

Now that you've vowed to abandon these totally untrue, unhealthy beliefs, it's time to really take a look at yourself in the mirror. No, you're not looking to find wrinkles, blemishes, cellulite, or other imperfections in your appearance. Rather, you're looking to see how you mess up your chances of finding Mr. Right.

Quite frankly, even though the chump you've dumped behaved like a jerk, you must accept the fact that you allowed him to treat you this way. While he holds the weight of the responsibility in terms of his bad behavior, he wouldn't have gotten away with it unless he'd had a willing participant. I know it's hard to admit, but you allowed yourself to be a captive audience. And you emotionally blackmailed yourself into staying loyal to him, even while you recognized that he was Mr. Wrong. Actually, your biggest mistake was in not seeing the choices you had—namely, that you always had the option to leave once it got bad. (You are like Dorothy in *The Wizard of Oz*, who had the power to go back home anytime she wanted; she just didn't believe in herself enough.) If you really want to attract Mr. Right, you must accept your responsibility for your choices and stop seeing yourself as a victim! You must accept your screwups and assert your power to choose.

Of course, I'm not advocating premature departure, or PD. The PD syndrome is the result of a pendulum swing common to people who have lived a life of extremes. They need to go to the other extreme before balancing out in the middle. In other words, because you now fully recognize you overextended your stay in this past relationship, you're likely to be very vigilant to any bad treatment and may dump a future relationship hastily. You may perceive any treatment that's not perfect to be in the same ballpark as the behavior of the chump. So I'm just warning you to be careful not to overgeneralize and start booting out all potential suitors just because you think they'll all end up just like the jerk. All men aren't chumps!

Face it, you've been a chump-dweller—that is, a woman who's allowed herself to stay with someone who treats her badly, who forsakes her own happiness, and who stays stuck feeling bad. Notice I use the past tense here—you've *been*, not *are*. I'm sure you're onto my tactics by now. I want you to see this as something you're over and done with, or at least in the process of getting rid of. You must no longer accept this as your identity.

I highlight your chump-dweller potential to empower you,

not to shame you. With conscious awareness, you can make different choices next time. And remember, you're in good company. Millions of women, even those of great status, qualify as chump-dwellers. But you know how much this hurts you, so it's time to cross over to the land of the good-guy-dweller!

Once again it's time to pull out your journal and make an extensive list of all the ways you sabotage your love-life happiness. Really give this some deep thought. If you truly want to escape the lair of another chump, you must acknowledge your issues. While this may not be the most pleasant exercise, it's well worth your time and energy.

Though I wish I could offer you a generic list of sabotaging behaviors, we women are ever so clever at coming up with unique ways to deviate from a positive path. So while I can't give you a precise definition or definitive criteria, I've included what I see as common dynamics shared by recovering chump-dwellers. So use the following as a guide, but do personalize it.

+ I'm prone to seeing myself as a victim, even when I have choices.
+ I stay far too long in situations that aren't good for me.
+ I tend to dismiss obvious red flags, hoping that I will be able to change my man's negative behavior.
+ I don't take my needs seriously enough.
+ I have holes in my self-esteem and hence don't value myself enough.

Once you've identified your own sabotaging attitudes, beliefs, or behaviors, you can change them into positive goals. For instance, you can change "I'm prone to seeing . . ." to "I will honor that I always have choices, even if I don't like the options I have." The key is to embrace the fact that it is your job to fix whatever is broken. Don't hold anyone else accountable for your mistakes.

Elena was plagued by a victim mentality. She experienced chronic feelings of hurt and betrayal, not only in her intimate relationships but with just about everyone. True, she had actually been victimized by her parents, having never received love and attention and having been physically abused by both. But it simply wasn't true that everyone in her life as an adult had a mission to harm her. Yet since she experienced the world through the eyes of a wounded child, she often failed to see the many options she had to take better care of herself. Rather, she frequently flocked to relationships with men who took her for granted and didn't understand that she didn't have to be a prisoner. Fortunately, Elena tossed her victim mentality right out the window and as a result became far more empowered to make healthier choices.

Of course it may take you awhile to fully put into practice these new declarations. But if you keep practicing, you'll see progress. And you'll feel a lot more confident as well.

Living in the Here-and-Now and Losing Regrets

You can cook up a surefire recipe for anxiety or despair by doing something, discovering that the "something" proved not to be in your best interests, and then regretting it. In other words, you make a choice, conscious or otherwise, it doesn't work out the way you hoped or planned, and then you drive yourself nuts with statements like, "If only I had done x, y, or z" or "If only I hadn't done a, b, or c."

Ruminating about moments already passed leaves you with a sense of hopelessness and helplessness because you have no control over anything that's already transpired. No matter how much you may desire to roll back the clock, you simply can't change the past. So whether you wasted six months, six years, or six decades of your life, there's nothing you can do about that now. But you sure as heck can do something about the present because you have a lot of power over how you create and experience your life in the here-and-now.

Everyone makes mistakes. Unless you have found the secret to absolute perfection, you will make them, too. The trick, however, to ensuring your happiness is to acknowledge your mistakes and work toward not making the same ones over and over again. But you can't move forward if you cry over spilled milk. So rather than living in regret, learn from your mistakes and take action to change the things that drive you down dead-end roads.

Keep a particularly close eye out for moments when you ponder the "should haves," "would haves," and "could haves." These will get you nowhere. Instead, focus on setting up goals to make the necessary changes. Doing so will empower you to avoid making the same mistakes over and over again.

Gretchen, a four-time chump-lover, really hit the wall after dumping Kyle. A pure snake-type, Kyle had played every con in the book with Gretchen. He stole from her, forged checks, and lied to her constantly about everything. But she loved the guy, and it broke her heart to face the fact that he was such a loser. Despite his repeated bad behavior, she had stayed with him for more than five years. At thirty-seven, she faced the prospect of never being able to have her own biological children, realizing that it would probably take another couple of years to meet the right guy, get married, and begin a family. Sure, she could always adopt, but this alternative didn't ease the loss she felt.

Gretchen had a heck of a time letting go of regrets. She didn't have any trouble owning her responsibility for how she got herself into this mess to begin with. But she was completely entrenched in trying to turn back the clock, hoping to recover what she'd wasted by living in fantasyland. What she needed to do instead was grieve her loss and then open her eyes to real possibilities in the present. Gretchen eventually came to trust that she could make her life better, even though she could never recapture her thirties. Once she came to appreciate that she couldn't reclaim time lost, she felt much better. Within a year, she'd recovered quite nicely. At times she got a bit discouraged, having continued to meet lots of losers. But eventually she met a great guy. Though I haven't heard from her since, I have a pretty good guess that this one turned out to be Mr. Right.

Now it's your turn. What regrets are you still harboring? Are you ready to let them go? Go on, give it a try. There's only an upside to letting bygones be bygones. For one, you'll feel much better. Two, your self-esteem will improve since you won't also be bogged down by all the guilt and shame that often go hand in hand with regret. And three, you'll have much more energy to put into making a better future for yourself.

Write down in detail all of your regrets. Then burn the paper and say good-bye to them. Whenever your mind tries to push you back in the direction of regret, say these words in your head: "Thanks, but no thanks. I'd rather save my energy for constructive changes in the present." Take the information you learned from the regret and ask yourself what you need to do differently to avoid making the same mistake. Then create a plan of action and apply it!

Quick Recipe Guide
for Step Six

- ✦ Identify any negative myths you believe about being a woman.
- ✦ Change these myths into positive statements.

Accepting Your Own Screwups

✦ Practice rehearsing aloud at least five positive statements about being you! Say these several times per day, and if you can muster up the courage, tell them to a friend or two as well. The more we put out positive energy, the more likely we are to receive it back!

✦ Make a list of the mistakes you've made and work on accepting them without shaming or blaming yourself. Use compassion and empathy. Continue practicing all you learned about self-lovin'. Now, if ever, you need it most of all.

✦ Openly acknowledge the mistakes you've made. Tell a close friend or family member what you're learning about yourself. This will help you get rid of any traces of shame. It might seem awkward at first, but practicing open disclosure deepens your sense of responsibility.

✦ Identify the things you regret. Remind yourself over and over again that regret gets you nowhere. Instead dedicate all your energy to creating positive change.

✦ Make a list of at least five goals for behavioral or attitude change and a plan for how to implement them. For instance, you may discover you need to become more attentive to how you feel in an interaction and less servicing of others. In other words, you are a people-pleaser, and not being more attentive to yourself has caused you to dismiss some really big red flags when you signed up to be with the former chump. So you will practice asking yourself every fifteen minutes or so, "How am I feeling right now?" Then you note the emotion and decide whether you should continue the interaction or set a boundary. You can practice this with anyone, the checker at the grocery store or the random stranger you exchange small talk with in the elevator. The more you check in with your feelings, the better you'll become at weeding out the chumps from the good guys.

Chapter 11

{ *step seven* }

Time to Party—Be the Birthday Girl

Okay, so it's not your real birthday. Who cares? You can celebrate anyway. In fact, this doctor orders you to participate in a full-blown, deluxe, self-indulgence package! No, you don't have to max out your budget (or you might cause a whole other set of problems), but I strongly encourage you to begin engaging in guilt-free frivolous fun—immediately. You must learn how to treat yourself as if you are the birthday girl, even if it's not your real birthday. I'm not suggesting you become a narcissist. But chances are you underindulge in being the center of attention. Hence, you need to create a new balance. Swing the pendulum and practice being much more celebratory, with *you* as the object of the celebration.

However, before you can fully enjoy your pseudo-birthday-girl status, you must adopt a positive attitude and work toward actively breaking all associations you're still holding onto that involve memories of the chump. You must reclaim all places you and the chump went to and the activities you did and reestablish them as neutral territory. So let's get started right away with developing a positive attitude—or, as I prefer to call it, "turning chicken shit into chicken salad."

Turning Chicken Shit into Chicken Salad

You may prefer the phrase "turning lemons into lemonade," but I like the chicken salad metaphor better, as it makes an even more powerful statement about how you can transform just about anything into something positive. I'm not endorsing a Pollyanna existence, where you act as if everything were rosy, even when it truly sucks. Nor am I suggesting you live in denial. But more often than not, if we rearrange our perception, we can find a silver lining in many situations that may seem bleak at first glance. If you take on a glass-half-empty approach to life, you're bound to be more pessimistic, whereas if you adopt the glass-half-full stance, you will feel more optimistic. The reality remains the same, but you will feel better in it, and hence create a positive spiral.

Understandably after the loss of a relationship, you're bound to feel as if the glass is pretty dry, even if the guy you lost is a chump. But this isn't mandatory. You can just as easily shift your perspective to seeing the gains rather than the losses. And even further, when you perceive a situation from a negative perspective, as in the half-empty approach, you're more focused on what you don't have, and it's harder to see a way out. From the half-full perspective, you'll see yourself as far closer to your goal even though the reality is the same. Plus, with positive energy, you can embrace that you have the power to fill up the glass all the way to the top and have the relationship you desire. So it's time you made this shift, if you haven't already done so. You simply can't expect to have a happy love life if you walk around with a negative or pessimistic attitude.

To create a positive attitude, you have to shake off any doom and gloom residue. Begin by paying attention to any thoughts of hopelessness or despair and revise these into hopeful ones. For example, let's say you have plans with a friend and she has to break them because her beau needs her help with something. Given that you've been mending from a recent breakup, you're likely to be upset that your friend won't be available as you had planned. You might even be angry with her or resent the fact that she actually has a boyfriend and you don't. It might then be tempting to sit around and pout for the evening, feeling sorry for yourself.

But how would any of these responses help you? The answer is they wouldn't. In fact, having any of the above responses would simply make you feel worse. So what would be the point?

A positive response to the above scenario would be, "Oh well. I was really looking forward to spending time with my friend, but since that is no longer possible, I'll fill the time with something else I might enjoy." Don't sit around feeling bad; instead be proactive and assert other available options. Get on the phone and make new plans. Or use the free time to do something you've been unable to find the time for. This would be a glass-half-full response.

I'm not suggesting you disguise your true feelings. Quite the contrary. It's fine to feel the full range of emotions. But it won't serve you well to dwell on negative feelings, particularly when you have the power to change your perspective and help yourself feel better.

Most important, don't see yourself as a victim. Nothing has

been done to you that you haven't allowed. And now you're *choosing* to make room for a far better relationship. And that's a very smart, positive, and self-caring choice!

Now it's time to reframe your lost relationship with the chump with a glass-half-full approach. You absolutely must do this before you can have a fresh start at a new relationship. If you carry over negative energy, you'll be a nightmare for someone to date, let alone become intimate with. Using what you've already learned thus far about taking responsibility for your own choices, write out at least a couple of paragraphs that describe the course of the relationship, why it went south, and what you've learned that will help you have a better relationship the next time around. Below is an example:

> *Last year when I met Lance, I felt particularly vulnerable after having quit my job and lost my cat. My self-esteem was in the toilet, and Lance seemed to be the answer to my prayers. But what I wasn't aware of was that when I'm feeling good about myself, I don't really like to be rescued. I have my own opinions about things and I like to be respected for my point of view. I morphed myself to Lance's personality and gave up many of my own needs and preferences for fear of being alone in my grief.*
>
> *While Lance took advantage of my vulnerability, it was I who allowed him to do so. I didn't speak up and resented him for not figuring out what I needed. I can see now how I'm responsible for my own choice to have stayed far too long in this relationship. I'm glad to be out of that relationship so that I can finally have the opportunity to spread my wings and hold out for someone who will embrace my gifts.*

Dump That Chump!

The goal of this exercise is to help you get rid of excess baggage once and for all. The good guys out there won't be attracted to a woman who feels victimized and doesn't claim her own choices. So if you don't get rid of the negative attitude, you're bound to either pair up with another chump or, at the very least, someone who also blames others for his issues. And to have a solid, healthy relationship, both people need to take responsibility for their own lives. Then a couple can truly THRIVE!

Breaking Mental Ties

Not surprisingly, many women resist leaving icky relationships, not just because they really love the guy they're with, but because they've come to associate so much of their daily life with him. Hence, they falsely believe they won't enjoy these same places and activities, once experienced as a couple, without him. They have Thursday morning coffee at Starbucks, Friday night drinks at the local pub, Saturday jogs at the local park, and Sunday night reality shows—all tied up with memories of him.

One woman I worked with had taken up skydiving to please her boyfriend and become his adventure-buddy. She discovered she loved it! But he turned out to be a big chump, and she finally mustered up the guts to leave him. But she also mistakenly dumped her newfound favorite activity as well, only adding insult to injury. Thankfully, she came to recognize that the sky was big enough for both of them and she could continue to enjoy the sport.

Following a breakup, the places and activities associated with the chump become taboo because you're too afraid to reexperience painful memories of him. Not to mention, you might run into him. And up until now, I've encouraged you not to go to these places or do these things. But now it's time to shift. Again using an analogy of a smoker trying to quit who forgoes the morning java to keep from inhaling those toxic sticks, you believe you must forgo previous pleasures in order to minimize the memories of the chump. But this becomes very self-defeating, giving him far more power than he deserves and making your own world smaller and smaller. That's enough to make anyone depressed. But it doesn't have to be this way.

Once you start revisiting these places, getting rid of trace memories of the chump, you can make new memories, independent of him. Hey, the chump doesn't own your favorite places, nor does he hold the rights to the activities you once enjoyed together. You can make these your own again. With the right mind-set, you can start enjoying these same places and activities (P&A's) without him. And eventually you'll make new associations, not even giving him a second thought.

As I've made crystal clear, I'm no stranger to the pain of breaking up with a chump. I've had more than my fair share of such experiences. One of the most important lessons I learned through these gruesome times was not giving my feelings power over my actions; that is, not allowing fear to rule my world. Even though I may have *felt* I couldn't enjoy life without the chump, that didn't mean it was actually true. I had to rethink this and decide, "Maybe if I try, I can overcome my fears." And this turned out to be quite true. Much to my surprise, I've successfully reengaged in many P&A's once I reclaimed them as my own, such as skiing, camping, eating out at certain restaurants, and traveling to particular cities once solely associated with a guy. And you can, too!

If you've been avoiding your favorite P&A's for fear of coming face to face with the chump or of reexperiencing painful memories, it's time to move through them. Take off your running shoes, slow down, and face the fear. There's nothing dangerous about bumping into him. Remember: you don't want him anymore. And if you have a resurgence of painful memories, you now have plenty of tools to soothe yourself through the discomfort. Plus, if you really can't take it, you always have the option to leave and try again later. Often the first visit is the hardest, then it gets easier and easier. Remember, you have choices about how you feel!

So now it's time to make your P&A list. Write down every place and activity you've been avoiding, because you've feared either running into the chump or reexperiencing painful memories. Pick one item off your list and make a plan to reclaim the place or activity. Make this an ongoing exercise until you've successfully created new experiences for each item on your list.

This particular exercise has no time frame. Depending on how long your list is and how much of your life you spent with the chump, this may take quite awhile. Plus, you may never be able to recapture all the P&A's for any number of reasons—it would be too costly, take too much time, or you may no longer have any real interest in some of the things once specifically associated with the chump. For instance, you may have taken a lavish trip to Europe and you have no desire to go back there. That's fine. The key, however, is that you choose not to revisit because you no longer want to, not because you fear memories or bumping into the chump. Hence, if you still love to travel, you can always explore new places.

While this process will be ongoing, the goal for right now is simply to start with something. Maybe you'll go back to a restaurant where the two of you used to eat, but you'll order something you never dared because it was too expensive or too fattening. Or you'll rent the favorite movie you once watched together, only this time you'll invite a bunch of girlfriends over for a slumber party with lots of popcorn and sodas. Just switch it up enough so that you're doing what you used to do with him, but creating a new experience. Once you get one success under your belt, it will become much easier to continue this process with other items on your list.

Be careful not to pick something too special or you might freak yourself out and not trust that you can pull this off. I suggest you start with a more benign, less loaded item, and then move toward the more difficult, intense ones. For instance, you might first revisit your local café before you attempt to travel to the place where he proposed. Don't be discouraged if your first attempt does in fact bring along what you fear: a resurgence of painful memories or a lapse into missing him. Just let the feelings and thoughts pass through you without giving them any power. Say to yourself, "I can do this and enjoy it, if I so choose."

Elizabeth learned how to sail while she was dating Ted, an avid sportsman. She loved every minute of their time together on the water. In fact, it was during their sailing adventures that Elizabeth and Ted seemed like the perfect couple. And she cherished every moment they shared doing this activity. But while they got along great while dancing with the sea on a twenty-five-foot catamaran, they experienced little in common anywhere else. Turned out Ted was a control freak. While Elizabeth didn't mind him taking charge on the water (since she was the novice sailor), she couldn't stand his need to dominate in their day-to-day existence. And as she became better at maneuvering the boat, she also became less okay with his pushy behavior while sailing.

When Elizabeth eventually dumped Ted, she also sadly swore off sailing. She believed she could never again enjoy the waters unless Ted was by her side, even though she recognized he was a chump. But once she started practicing the Dump That Chump program, she found she didn't need Ted after all in order to enjoy sailing. And, rather than pine for Ted, who treated her like crap most of the time, she joined an athletic singles club where she could find new companions. And much to her surprise, she discovered lots of other avid sailors, even a few really cute ones. Before you know it, she was doing the very thing she thought she'd never again enjoy!

So take action now and reclaim your favorite P&A's.

Party-Girl Time

Once you make a decision to reclaim the P&A's originally shared with the chump, you become free to celebrate yourself in the world, with no restrictions. You no longer have to avoid places or people, and you can move freely about in your daily life.

Think of an image of yourself as a happy birthday girl, either from childhood or adulthood. What does this picture look like? I hope you're laughing, smiling, and playing. You feel free and alive and you love the attention. Think of this image for a moment and really let yourself enjoy it. Revisit this image in your mind several times a day, and use it as your guide for this step. If you can't recall an image of yourself as the happy birthday girl, use someone else as a model.

You can do all sorts of things as the birthday girl. Most important, I encourage you to throw a party for yourself. Go all out with party favors, decorations, and balloons. Ask others for their help. Make it a potluck dinner party, so you don't have to do all the work. Get a cake with *I've Dumped the Chump* written on it and put on tons of candles to blow out. Breaking free from a chump is a big event, so make it grand, but within your budget.

As an added bonus, pick something special you will do for yourself every day this week. Again, it doesn't have to be expensive, but it must be in honor of *you*. Let people know you are celebrating your accomplishment of dumping the chump. My guess is that your friends will welcome the opportunity to participate in your self-indulgence. They've probably become tired of only hearing you complain about being so unhappy and will lavish in your positive energy.

When you practice being the birthday girl, you must give it your all. Move outside of the box. If you've been isolating and feeling sorry for yourself, make a commitment to stop hiding and start living. There are all sorts of ways to play out being the birthday girl. Be creative. Say hi to strangers, put a little extra bounce in your step, and blow off trivial annoyances of daily life. Call friends, set up lunches, visit a museum. Do what's fun for you. All the while, remember you deserve to have a wonderful life, but you must make it that way. No one will hand you happiness on a silver platter. So don't wait around for others to pull you out of your funk. Instead, pull yourself out and go for it.

Also practice smiling whenever and wherever you can. Granted, if you should receive news of a true tragedy it wouldn't be appropriate to smile. But you'd be surprised at how often you would show your pearly whites if you simply changed your perspective on a situation. And believe it or not, smiling and laughing can actually have a positive effect on brain chemistry, creating a feedback loop where happy begets more happy begets more happy!

Quick Recipe Guide for Step Seven

✦ Practice making a conscious effort to indulge yourself. Be self-focused and make your happiness a top priority. You don't have to be demanding of others because you're going to provide your own supplies. But give your own self 100 percent of your energy.

✦ Plan your "I've Dumped the Chump" party. Decide on format, set the date, and make the calls for the invites.

✦ Start practicing turning chicken shit into chicken salad. Reframe negatives into positives and write out your glass-half-full statement concerning your past relationship. Feel free to do this for any other chumps you've dumped, just in case you're still holding onto old negative feelings from these relationships as well.

✦ Write out your P&A list. Then go through and prioritize which ones you can tackle first. Make a plan to revisit at least one item on the list as soon as possible.

✦ Implement the item you've chosen on your P&A list. It doesn't matter whether it's a weekend or weekday. Don't put this off or make excuses why you can't make this happen. Contrary to popular belief, time doesn't heal all wounds. Time can help, but only if we're doing something constructive and active while time passes by. You won't conquer your fears by passively waiting for another day to pass by. Be brave and take action, even if it's just grabbing a coffee where the two of you used to go and spending fifteen minutes sipping it while reading your favorite magazine.

✦ Go out and get your party supplies. Or if you feel particularly creative, make your own decorations.

✦ Party, party, party. Have fun. Enjoy yourself. Breathe in life and exhale whatever holds you back. The world is your oyster. Go out and pick a strand of pearls!

Chapter 12

{ step eight }

Sexy and Single—But No Sex!

Before we go any further, give yourself several pats on the back. You're doing great! If you've been diligently following the program, you should be well on your way to feeling much better than you felt at the onset. If you have hit some rough spots causing you to stray now and again, you may not be feeling as positive and hopeful as you could be, but you'll get there eventually. Remember, this isn't a race or a contest; you need to go at your own pace. Whatever you do, don't get down on yourself. As long as you keep trying, you're going to make headway!

Most important, stay with the glass half-full attitude and focus on your progress, not your setbacks. Of course, it's quite possible you chose to read this book in its entirety before attempting to actually follow the program. So you may not be experiencing much benefit since you haven't yet embarked on the actions recommended. No worries. That's totally fine! Just know you have a lot to look forward to.

This step covers claiming your feminine power and practicing being friendly and flirty. You're not yet ready to date; nor are you ready for anything actually sexual. But you can certainly begin to practice laying on the charm and becoming open to new attractions.

Claiming Your Feminine Power—It's Diva Time!

Girlfriend, listen up! Women have enormous power! We rock! And I'm sure the last time you checked, you reaffirmed that you are, in fact, a woman ☺. So if you want to attract Mr. Right, you must embrace this reality and claim the diva within you. I'm not suggesting you exploit your inherent power. Rather, be aware of it and don't push it away. Otherwise you're bound to minimize your importance yet again and be far more likely to end up with another chump. And we've already firmly established that your chump-dwelling days are over.

One of the realities women often don't understand is that many guys evolve into chumps because their own emotional bruises cause them to be terribly threatened by the power inherent in women. They perceive femininity as a threat to their masculinity, as if only one "inity" can exist. Many of these guys have what's known in my trade as an "inferiority complex," a fancy name that essentially means feeling like crap deep down inside. To cover up their sense of inadequacy, some chumps use the disguise of superiority, acting as if they believe they are way better than women. These guys unconsciously believe they can't preserve their masculinity without suppressing a woman's power. Believe it or not, most chumps aren't vicious sociopaths. Rather, they're terribly insecure, immature creatures, unable to be real men.

In contrast, the Mr. Rights of the world feel confident in themselves. They're not threatened by the power of femininity. They make room for both masculine and feminine energy. Because of their confidence (not to be confused with arrogance), they're able to enjoy and cherish a woman, thus having no need to put down her strength and vibrancy.

Chumps also often have problems embracing a woman who enjoys her sexuality. If a woman feels completely comfortable with herself and her body, a chump fears she will eventually discover she doesn't need him. Because he feels inadequate beneath his arrogant veneer, he believes that if a woman doesn't need him, she'll leave him. So he becomes compelled to put her down and keep her feeling inadequate so she'll remain dependent on him. Confident, healthy guys have no need to do this. They actually prefer a woman who enjoys her own sexuality.

By the way, feminine diva energy doesn't equate with passivity or docility. Rather it embodies strength as well as forthrightness. Whereas chumps tend to label women who have a backbone as bitches, the Mr. Rights see strong women as beautiful and alluring. So what's a woman to do? The answer: claim your femininity through loving your body, embracing your strength, and enjoying your sexuality.

Loving Your Body

We women notoriously attack our bodies, constantly focusing on all our imperfections. We do the very thing to ourselves that we've allowed the chump to do to us. We constantly put ourselves down and pick on various body parts. But this is no way for a woman to act! You simply must overcome any body insecurities or obsessions, and embrace the physique you've been given. Granted, if you tend to be unhealthily skinny or overweight, you would do yourself good to strive for a more healthy body. But please do this from the frame of mind of self-improvement, not from a place of self-hatred or from believing you're inadequate or unlovable.

Contrary to popular belief, many guys aren't looking for a supermodel. In fact, guys who genuinely appreciate women and who can participate in a healthy relationship don't even notice the flaws we tend to harp on. That doesn't mean that every guy (as well as every gal) won't have his physical preferences. But good guys have a balance between holding out for both physical and mental attraction. Good guys love women who enjoy their own bodies, regardless of shape or size. Women who embrace their bodies exude intoxicating sensuality. They're very appealing. It simply isn't true that only the waif-thin women (with miraculously disproportionately large boobs) get all the good guys. Women of all sizes, shapes, ages, and hair colors can have wonderful relationships with desirable men.

Loving your body requires embracing your total physical being as well as all of its functions. It means enjoying your curves, accepting cellulite, and appreciating the accumulating laugh lines. Loving your body also means honoring its abilities. Your body allows you to do all sorts of wonderful things: to dance, to sing, to feel pain or joy, to shiver, to tighten or loosen. The body is like an orchestra performing a beautiful symphony. You should revel in its wonder.

I know, you're probably thinking, "Is this doc nuts or what?" You're doing everything in your mind to negate the value of your particular body, in its shape and form. But, hey—I don't buy it and you shouldn't either. As someone who's suffered eating disorders (both bulimia and anorexia), I know what it's like to attack your own physique. No matter what you think, your body, whatever its dimensions, has tremendous value to you, and you must honor and cherish it!

I'm certainly not saying I've got this whole body image thing licked. I, too, sometimes resort to negative self-talk. But, all in all, I can tell you that it feels a heck of a lot better to enjoy what I have than to focus on what I'm lacking.

If you have trouble reveling in your body, try the following exercise. It might seem crazy, but please give it a go. Get naked with yourself!

Take your clothes off (in an appropriate time and place of course) and stand in front of the mirror buck-naked. No groaning about what you see. Instead, look at yourself with complete admiration and gratitude for the life-force within you. Next, select a body part you're most likely to pick on or criticize and do the opposite—instead praise your beauty. For instance, if you think you have a big butt, put your hands right on your derriere and give it a good squeeze, saying "Thank goodness for this tush. Were it not for you, I wouldn't be able to sit comfortably or fill out my jeans." Practice this exercise over and over again. Each time, select a different body part until you can stand tall, looking at your entire image in awe!

Embracing Your Strength

As the saying goes, "Whatever doesn't kill you, makes you stronger." It's true. You've been through a lot, and not only have you survived, but you're now well on the way to thriving. Don't underestimate your power to recover and move forward.

Make a list of all the hardships you've been able to overcome, including fears you've conquered and losses you've suffered. Enduring difficult situations actually strengthens your capacity for empathy and compassion. Use your list to remind you that you can get through anything if you put your mind to it!

Enjoying Your Sexuality

Learning to love your body and embrace your strength will help you to fully enjoy your sexuality. But you also need to examine any hang-ups or negative messages you carry around concerning your sexuality. Our society can be very repressive and oppressive when it comes to sexuality, particularly with women. We hear crap like "Nice girls don't talk about sex" or "Good girls don't have sex until marriage." Mind you, if you have any religious beliefs that dictate your sexual life, then I certainly don't mean to trample on your values. But do try to examine any subconscious messages that might be holding you back from expressing your sexuality and sensuality. Spend time this week exploring all your senses—tasting, smelling, touching, hearing, and seeing everything with great intensity. Take a bubble bath and then lavish your body with lotion, feeling your fingers massaging every inch of you. Enjoy the simple pleasures of life. Stop and smell the flowers, allow the taste of rich, dark chocolate to linger on your tongue, or feel the sun kissing your skin (with sunscreen on, of course). Run your fingers through your hair, noticing its texture. Turn the music up extra loud and feel the beat moving through your whole body.

These are just a few examples of the thousands of things you can do to heighten your sensuality. Be creative—the more in tune you are with your senses the more accessible your sexuality becomes.

Make a list of any hang-ups you have and vow to get rid of them. They serve no purpose but to hold you back from fully enjoying your feminine power. If the chump added to your woes in this area, stop giving him this power. Chances are if he put you down in this area, he was camouflaging his own insecurities. If you do in fact have some sexual hang-ups that make you a poor lover, do something constructive about it. There are lots of books that can help you understand how the body works and different methods to turn on a mate (and yourself). Don't feel bad, just take action to correct whatever the problem is.

If you've been raped or molested, you may need professional help. These types of violations can really mess with your head as well as create deep disturbance in your body. Don't let past trauma zap your energy in the present. Meet the traumas head-on and heal them so you can fully reclaim your body!

Practice Flirting

Many men are attracted to women who would not be considered objectively beautiful. In fact, lots of guys would take an average-looking woman with a great, dynamic personality over a gorgeous supermodel who doesn't know her butt from her forehead. And while a great ass or great pair of legs may command extra hoots, men are even more seduced by a woman with a great smile!

So from here forward, put on your happiest mood and practice flirting. Don't pick on the guys you know to be married or involved with someone. After all, you wouldn't want to create negative karma. But do notice men you find attractive and be extra friendly. Make the effort to smile, say hi, bat your eyelashes, and ask a curious question or two.

If you get the brush-off, don't take it personally. Everyone you find attractive won't necessarily reciprocate the same feelings. Or you might catch a guy in a bad mood. This exercise isn't about getting a date. It's just a way to spread your wings and get your feet wet, back in the pool of relationship opportunities. If you happen to meet someone you simply can't resist going out with, then go for it. But whatever you do, don't have sex. This will completely cloud your judgment and set you back to square one!

Quick Recipe Guide for Step Eight

✦ Identify all the ways in which you've been brainwashed to reject your feminine power.

✦ Practice loving your body, using the "get naked" mirror exercise.

✦ Identify all of the strengths and hardships you've overcome. Tack this on your wall where you can see it whenever you're feeling subpar.

✦ Create a list of sensual pleasures and start putting them into action.

✦ Practice flirting.

You go, girl! Embrace your femininity and shine!

Chapter 13

Teaming Up with Cupid

*Y*ou've arrived at your TGIF moment. If you've been following the program, you should be feeling free and clear of all the baggage that came along with being a chump-dweller. If you're pain-free, then you have the green light to put yourself back out there and have another go at love and romance. But this time you should be fully equipped with a finely polished chump-radar! Should you spot any signs of chumpiness, you now know to run for the hills.

Taking the plunge back into the dating world can be a bit scary for many women. The longer you've been out of it, the more intimidating it can be, especially since dating opportunities have changed so much over the past several years. Whereas setups and random meetings were once the main avenues for finding a love connection, you now have accessibility to umpteen online-dating sites, phone chat lines, and matchmaking services. And contrary to the once-popular belief that these alternative methods were strictly for losers and nerds, all these methods have their benefits, as long as you take precautions.

Being open-minded to multiple avenues increases your chances of finding Mr. Right. So don't let change or new possibilities scare you off. Take your time and do some research on the dating methods you prefer. Plus, at the end of the chapter, I'll give you some guidelines to these various avenues.

As you reapproach the dating scene, keep everything you've learned in the book close at hand, mainly continuing to practice good self-care and a positive attitude. You're in charge of your love life. Don't give this power away to luck or chance. And never again allow a guy to make you feel bad about yourself. The whole beauty of relationships is that healthy ones provide support and nurturance. From here forward, you must vow to make dating vacancies only for the truly awesome men who will cherish being with you. Don't set yourself up for more disappointment and rejection by settling for anything less.

If you've discovered that you still have holes in your self-esteem, don't do a date-dive quite yet. First get the help you need to fill up the holes. If you look toward another man to fill you up, you're headed for disaster once again. Confidence and good self-care are the essential ingredients to becoming a magnet for Mr. Right.

Granted, every intimate relationship has its ups and downs, even those with a good guy. No one is perfect. We all get grumpy and have bad days now and again. Sometimes our attraction to someone wanes, especially if we are coping with a lot of stress or if we have a big conflict to resolve. But in healthy relationships, the loving, positive feelings continue to resurface and grow stronger with time. The bond strengthens and the passion inevitably returns. Clearly, the better matched you are with someone from the get-go, the higher likelihood you'll land a successful relationship. So it's time to get smart with your heart!

Creating a Relationship Vision

We're all unique beings with different preferences. And as long as the things we desire in a mate aren't outlandish or too extensive, there's no reason to settle for less than you desire. For instance, if you're a very energetic person, you may desire a guy who enjoys a lot of activity. If you settle for a guy who moves at a slow pace, you'll be doing yourself a disservice. Or if the theater and arts draw your passion, you should definitely hold out for a guy who enjoys the same. On the other hand, if you have a list of non-negotiables the length of the Mississippi River, you're probably going to be single for a long time. So while I encourage you to be picky, please also recognize the importance of flexibility and compromise.

As a guideline, your list of nonnegotiable preferences should be up to about ten items. Then you can add other preferences where you'd be willing to compromise if the guy has most of what you're looking for in the nonnegotiable department. Be as specific as possible so you really have a clear picture of what suits you. Also, be especially careful not to include things that really don't matter in the long run when it comes to being a good relationship partner. For example, while you might wish to be with someone who is financially stable, holding out for a guy who drives a red Lamborghini with a tan interior wouldn't do much to help insure a solid relationship. So be reasonable! (Of course, if he happens to drive a Lamborghini and he meets all the other criteria, you certainly don't have to rule him out! ☺)

Using the list you've just created and the list you developed in Chapter Seven, "Redefining You," begin creating your relationship vision. Make categories for both nonnegotiable and negotiable preferences. Don't place any restrictions on yourself.

Put down everything that comes to mind. After you're all done, go back and revisit each item and rank it on a scale of one to ten (with ten being an absolute necessity). Think about each item. Then cross off the ones that don't really matter to your ultimate happiness.

I've had to come face to face with my desire for lots of contact. Basically I'm what I call a contact-junky, in terms of both emotional intimacy and physical affection. I'm simply never going to do well in a relationship with someone who doesn't like to connect throughout the day by phone or e-mail when we're apart, and who loves to sit close by when we're sharing space. Except during times of unbearable heat waves, I prefer to be entwined like a pretzel with someone I love.

I used to think something was wrong with me for wanting to be so closely linked with an intimate partner. Some might even consider this codependency. But I would disagree, since I can continue to maintain my own identity and definitely have no trouble holding onto my own opinions, even with such closeness. So now I fully embrace my contact needs as one of my nonnegotiables, and I would never even consider having a partner who is more of a space-junky. I've certainly had my share of those types. And while they weren't all chumps, I wasn't happy.

Granted, such a close connection might feel entirely smothering to someone else. I know lots of women who would be annoyed or feel burdened by a guy who liked checking in on a regular basis. So this is not a mandatory criterion for all successful relationships. Rather, I'm simply highlighting how important it is to not shame yourself for your needs and preferences or deny them. It's about being in sync in areas that truly matter that determines compatibility.

Though I don't want to dictate what you put on your list,

there are a few areas that do seem to require high compatibility to increase the probability of having a long-lasting, healthy intimate relationship. So in addition to everything else you might think to put on your list, I suggest you also make sure you pay attention to the following items:

✦ Preferences for contact—i.e., how much time you like to spend by yourself versus how much time you enjoy dedicating to a mate and how close you prefer to be emotionally. Space-junkies and contact-junkies don't tend to mix well. (FYI, when you reenter the dating scene, don't use the first couple of dates as a barometer for how much contact your potential mate may desire. True preferences generally don't emerge until the initial electric shock starts to wear off. But you can find out a lot about someone's preferences by the way they talk about prior relationships. So when you start dating, don't be shy about asking for contact-preference history.)

✦ Sense of humor. If we don't find ourselves laughing at similar jokes and situations as our mate, we're likely to become resentful and possibly even offended. Humor is a very personal thing. This makes going to a comedy club together a good test of compatibility. Or, at the very least, buy a joke book and read it aloud. See what stuff you both laugh at.

✦ Religion or spiritual beliefs. I've worked with multiple couples who have considerably different religious and spiritual backgrounds and beliefs. This doesn't have to be a deal-breaker, but both people have to be very tolerant of differences in order to weather incompatibility in this area.

✦ Attitudes about having/raising children. If you have children or desire to be a parent at some point, it's critical to be compatible with a mate in this area. It's not like you can sort-of have kids or have half of one in case you don't want the full responsibility. So if you find a mate who doesn't want kids and you do, or vice versa, this will inevitably pose a serious problem. Also of equal importance is style of parenting. For instance, if you were spanked as a child and you believe this harmed you in some way, you're going to be adamantly opposed to spanking your child as a form of discipline. If you're with a guy who feels like a firm swat on the butt kept him in line, he might think spankings benefit children. And now you've waged war! Don't hook up with someone who has vastly different attitudes about raising kids unless the differences don't strike any important chords.

✦ Housekeeping. Being a lousy housekeeper doesn't make someone a chump or bad person. Some people simply weren't taught the importance of tidiness. Some suffer from ADD (attention-deficit disorder), making challenges of organization very difficult. Others like things clean, but they don't seem to mind living in messy surroundings. Others simply don't care about their surroundings or the property of others at all. Decide where you are on the continuum of tidiness and cleanliness and try to hold out for someone who is a good match. If you're the messy one, try to improve in this area before you embark on another relationship. And if you tend to be the tidier one in relationships, let go a little if you border on being compulsive. Whatever you do, don't settle for a pig-type chump—or you're going to have fantasies of slaughtering him when he leaves his dirty socks on top of your brand new purse. Of course, there's always the option of hiring someone else to do the cleaning!

✦ Importance of extended family relationships. Some people are really close to their families. That can be a blessing or a curse, depending on whether you share the same connection with your family. Also, if you don't like the extended family members of your mate, but he's close to them, you must recognize that your attempts to get in between these relationships would most likely result in defensiveness on his part and frustration on yours. Again, not a deal-breaker, but something to keep in mind as a potential sore spot, should you attach to someone with big differences in this area.

✦ Preferences for how to spend leisure time. Ideally, assuming you're not a workaholic, most likely you have several hours per week for downtime. Some people like to jump out of planes or climb Mt. Everest as their playtime activity, whereas others prefer lounging on the beach sipping Mai Tais. One form of play isn't better than another; they just express different levels of energy. If you take a high-energy person and pair him/her with more of a relaxer-type, you're bound to get friction. If a couple can enjoy both ends of the spectrum, then it's quite workable. But it can be like trying to mix oil and water if the couple has two dominantly different ideas about what's fun to do. So unless you pair together two highly independent, space-junky types, being too different in this area may leave you feeling quite disappointed.

✦ Work ethic. Some people place a very high value on status, wealth, and climbing the corporate ladder. Others understand the need to be productive, but they place a much higher value on working to live rather than living to work. Some people take off work at even the slightest sniffle, pampering themselves to prevent a cold. Others wouldn't consider missing a day of work, unless they were either on their deathbed or the victim of some unforeseen circumstance, like a flat tire, prohibiting them from getting there. And these types would probably get on the phone anyway and continue the workday, while handling the obstacle. Some people toss their cell phones on the counter after work, not to be reclaimed until the next day. Others have it constantly dangling from an ear. Again, no wrong or right here. Just keep these differences in mind when thinking about the type of mate you desire.

There are all sorts of other things that could pose problems in a relationship, so don't restrict yourself to the ones I've included. You may know of other important areas specific to your prior experiences. So make sure to include whatever you deem important to you. After all, it's your love life you're dealing with, not someone else's. Plus, don't skimp on the energy you apply to this exercise. Be thoughtful and attentive to the things that matter to you. Don't do it all in one sitting. This should be something you think about over a couple of days and add to. Later, you might delete some items that seem trivial. Also, when you're finished, run your vision by a close friend or two and get his/her opinion of how fitting it seems to you. Sometimes our friends have very valuable insights into our blind spots or self-distortions.

Once you've created your relationship vision, read it several times a day. Make sure it continues to fit what you desire, and modify it if it doesn't. Keep this handy and review it often. The more you live and breathe what you desire, the better your chances of bringing in your real-life prince!

Margot, a thirty-two-year-old fundraiser, had always been very successful in her career, but far less successful in the game of love. Like all the women described throughout the book, Margot was a chump-magnet, constantly getting hurt by no-good men. But Jarred, the worst of the bunch, was the final straw. With Jarred, Margot had almost sold her soul, and he would have taken her for everything she was worth had she not finally paid attention to the blazing red flags.

Fortunately, Margot escaped the lair of Jarred and managed

to recover to a level of basic functioning. She swore off men for about nine months and focused again on building her career. But, while her choice not to get back in the saddle served to keep her from getting hurt, it clearly wasn't what she wanted. She knew she'd never be happy as one of those women who never marry or have kids. She wanted both a husband and a few kids, and she certainly deserved to have her desires come true! But she was too darn afraid.

Thankfully, I was privileged to be able to help Margot before her renunciation of men became a permanent vow. We identified her internalized images of love, went through all the applicable exercises, and healed her broken heart. She established her relationship vision and became willing to venture back into the dating world. This time around, however, she became quite adept at seeing the writing on the wall and moving away from chumps rather than toward them. It was music to my ears when I heard from Margot about a year after she'd finished therapy that she was happily engaged to Mr. Right. Way to go, Margot!

Please use Margot's story and all the others in the book as inspiration for your own progress. These women have suffered just like you, but they've all been able to overcome their pain. Some have found their Mr. Right and others are still searching. But at least they all have hope and no longer settle for less than they deserve.

Doing the Dating Thing

Dating can be very difficult for many women. For those who truly desire to be in a long-term intimate relationship, the whole process may seem like a superficial waste of time. But if you reframe your perspective and instead view this phase as an essential component to developing a better picker, you'll value and enjoy the process much more.

Here are some tips to successful dating and ultimately landing Mr. Right:

✦ Take your time. Don't be in a hurry to jump back into a relationship right away.

✦ Be highly discriminating on the front end. As a friend of mine says, "Always ask yourself, what might bother you somewhere down the line?" Remember, people usually put their best foot forward at the beginning during the courtship phase. While much of what's presented may turn out to be the real thing, sometimes the glossy finish wears off and the picture in front of you isn't so pretty. Be alert to red flags and don't try to convince yourself that you can change someone into who you want them to be.

✦ Don't have sex with someone until you've decided you want to be in a relationship with him. Women notoriously have sex with guys before they're ready and then suffer all sorts of consequences, from feeling used to creating false intimacy. We can easily convince ourselves that we're in love with someone just because we've slept with him. It clouds our judgment. So don't jump in the sack until you're fairly certain he has "The One" potential.

✦ If you're attracted to a guy and think he might be worthy of a relationship with you, make sure you base this on having had a variety of experiences with him. In other words, if all you've ever done is have quiet dinners or gone bowling as a solo couple, you can't possibly know what kind of person he is. You have to do lots of different things, in a variety of situations. Meet his friends, check out how he lives, watch how he treats the person serving you food in the restaurant. Is he super-nice to you but talks badly about other people? Does he have temper tantrums when he doesn't get his way? Does he talk poorly about all his exes as though they were the demons and he was the saint? These would all be signals that you will someday also be the recipient of this bad behavior. So check him out in numerous contexts and see how he behaves. If he fits your criteria (which I hope by now are a much higher standard than before), then go ahead and give a relationship with him a whirl.

✦ Expect some disappointment. Remember: no one is perfect. You will see some flaws. Just decide whether these are flaws you can accept. Don't get trapped into "potential mentality"; that is, the belief that through your love you will change him into who you think he should be. You already know firsthand that doesn't work! Surely, people can make some minor adjustments and compromises in how they approach things, but most of the time what you see is what you'll get after the camouflaging wears off.

✦ If you date someone for a while and it's not going as you had hoped, get out sooner rather than later. If a guy stops calling or doesn't want to see you anymore, don't let this bruise your ego too much. You're better off without him. And definitely don't go chasing after him or try to convince him of why he should be with you. Just move on. If a guy doesn't want to be with you, he has every right to call it quits, just as you have a right to dismiss any suitors you don't care for. We can't be the object of every guy's desire!

✦ Be patient. The efforts you spend in taking your time will pay off tenfold in the long run and save you from ever having to go through the Dump That Chump program again.

Dating Resources

As you're probably well aware, you don't even have to leave your house anymore to meet someone you might wish to date. All you need is a telephone and/or a computer. If you look online or in the phone book, you'll discover pages upon pages of dating services, phone chat-lines, and matchmakers. While there are certainly some drawbacks to these methods, they can most definitely be a positive resource, often outweighing any negatives. So don't be intimidated. Be open-minded. Take your time and try many different avenues.

Below is a list of some of the drawbacks to alternative dating methods. Though keep in mind, with a different perspective a downside could actually be an upside.

- ✦ Still hold a bit of a stigma for some people. (Of course, who cares if you ultimately find Mr. Right!)
- ✦ Must take extra precautions concerning safety. Though in reality you don't really know the truth about anyone you've just met, regardless of whether you found him on an Internet dating site or walking through the vegetable section at the market. Even if you meet someone through a setup by a best friend, no one truly knows how the guy will be once he's part of an intimate couple.
- ✦ Can seem more distant and more mechanical than locking eyes with a stranger. But sometimes this is better, since Cupid can be very deceiving.
- ✦ People can become lazy and isolated—getting off on the search and then never ending up making an actual date. Of course, this one doesn't apply to matchmaking services requiring a face-to-face meeting.
- ✦ People often post distorted, unrealistic pictures or information about themselves and may be playing a game with no real interest in meet-

ing someone. Of course, people can do this in person as well. Though granted, with a face-to-face meeting, people can't distort how they look too much. (Though women do it all the time with makeup, tummy tucks, and pushup bras.)

The upside to alternate dating avenues includes:

- ✦ High accessibility. The Internet doesn't sleep—so you're not confined to searching at any particular time of day.
- ✦ Much larger pool to choose from.
- ✦ Reduced limitations of geography and meeting the right person at the right time.
- ✦ Assuming the person on the other end is being honest, you can get to know a fair amount about him before investing time and energy into going on an actual date.
- ✦ You don't have to dress up, look sexy, or do your makeup while searching online or connecting through a phone chat-line.
- ✦ You can do an Internet security background check on the person you might consider meeting.
- ✦ With dating services and matchmakers you get the benefit of their years of expertise in hooking up compatible people. Though these setups often don't work, at least you can avoid the awkward moments you have with friends when you don't really mesh with the guy he/she thought would be perfect for you. Plus, friends often have an agenda behind getting you to go out with someone they think is great for you, whereas people who run dating or matchmaking services will likely be more objective and less attached to the success of the setup. Of course, this isn't always the case. So do be sure to check out the service's reputation and references very carefully before signing up.

I'm not advocating one method over the other, just recommending you don't rule any avenue out prematurely. You might try one approach and decide it's really not for you—but you will have at least tried. For instance, there's a company that focuses on speed-dating, where you meet several people for a very short period of time and then decide which ones you might want to pursue. I've worked with people who find this to be a perfect match for their personality, whereas other, more traditional folks find this to be very unfulfilling. So give them all a shot and go for it!

Quick Recipe Guide for Step Nine

✦ Make your list of negotiables and nonnegotiables concerning qualities you're looking for in a mate.

✦ Work on developing your relationship vision.

✦ Look into different dating services. Research the ones you think would fit your personality. Consider signing up for a few. Plus, start putting the word out to trusted friends and family members that you're open to setups.

✦ Go out and celebrate! You've graduated from the Dump That Chump program. Congratulations!

As a final note: I wish you all the success in finding Mr. Right. You can do it. Always remember there's help out there if you need it. Just be good to yourself and honor your right to have a fulfilling love life.

Hugs and best wishes,
Dr. Debra